Surviving
Divorce

52 Brilliant Ideas

one good idea can change your life

Surviving Divorce

Your Roadmap Through the Emotional and Financial Maze

Victoria Perrett

A Perigee Book

A PERIGEE BOOK
Published by the Penguin Group
Penguin Group (USA) Inc.
375 Hudson Street, New York, New York 10014, USA
Penguin Group (Canada), 90 Eglinton Avenue East, Suite 700, Toronto, Ontario M4P 2Y3, Canada
(a division of Pearson Penguin Canada Inc.)
Penguin Books Ltd., 80 Strand, London WC2R oRL, England
Penguin Group Ireland, 25 St. Stephen's Green, Dublin 2, Ireland (a division of Penguin Books Ltd.)
Penguin Group (Australia), 250 Camberwell Road, Camberwell, Victoria 3124, Australia
(a division of Pearson Australia Group Pty. Ltd.)
Penguin Books India Pvt. Ltd., 11 Community Centre, Panchsheel Park, New Delhi—110 017, India
Penguin Group (NZ), Cnr. Airborne and Rosedale Roads, Albany, Auckland 1310, New Zealand
(a division of Pearson New Zealand Ltd.)
Penguin Books (South Africa) (Pty.) Ltd., 24 Sturdee Avenue, Rosebank, Johannesburg 2196, South Africa

Penguin Books Ltd., Registered Offices: 80 Strand, London WC2R oRL, England

While the author has made every efffort to provide accurate telephone numbers and Internet addresses at the time of publication, neither the publisher nor the author assumes any responsibility for errors, or for changes that occur after publication. Further, the publisher does not have any control over and does not assume any responsibility for author or third-party websites or their content.

SURVIVING DIVORCE

First American edition: January 2007
Originally published in Great Britain in 2005 by The Infinite Ideas Company Limited.

Perigee trade paperback ISBN: 978-0-399-53305-1

An application to register this book for cataloging has been submitted to the Library of Congress.

PRINTED IN THE UNITED STATES OF AMERICA

10   9   8   7   6   5   4   3   2   1

PUBLISHER'S NOTE: This publication is designed to provide accurate and authoritative information in regard to the subject matter covered. It is sold with the understanding that the publisher is not engaged in rendering legal, accounting, or other professional services. If you require legal advice or other expert assistance, you should seek the services of a competent professional.

Most Perigee Books are available at special quantity discounts for bulk purchases for sales promotions, premiums, fund-raising, or educational use. Special books, or book excerpts, can also be created to fit specific needs. For details, write: Special Markets, The Berkley Publishing Group, 375 Hudson Street, New York, New York 10014.

Brilliant ideas

Brilliant features

Each chapter of this book is designed to provide you with an inspirational idea that you can read quickly and put into practice right away.

Throughout you'll find four features that will help you to get right to the heart of the idea:

- *Here's an idea for you* Take it on board and give it a try—right here, right now. Get an idea of how well you're doing so far.

- *Try another idea* If this idea looks like a life changer then there's no time to lose. *Try another idea* will point you straight to a related tip to enhance and expand on the first.

- *Defining idea* Words of wisdom from masters and mistresses of the art, plus some interesting hangers-on.

- *How did it go?* If at first you do succeed, try to hide your amazement. If, on the other hand, you don't, then this is where you'll find a Q and A that highlights common problems and how to get over them.

Introduction

Divorce is traumatic. Divorce is hard. And, quite frankly, divorce hurts. If I were to say anything else it would simply be a blanket of words I'd woven to try and cover the facts. There is no question that going through a divorce is tough, but it doesn't have to be impossible.

As divorce rates soar worldwide, marital breakdown has become an issue that we can't afford to ignore. In fact, it's something that almost all of us will face at some stage in our lives, either with our own relationship or with those of friends and family. While this high growth rate of divorce is obviously a worrying issue that we as a society have to address, it does mean that there is more awareness and tolerance of the subject at every level.

Like all other major life events, divorce is a process. It has a beginning, a middle, and, thank goodness, an end. As you go through this process, your emotions, finances, and even health will come under fire. Some days you will feel positive, alive, and free; other days you'll feel utterly dreadful. The key thing is not to panic when you do have a bad day.

This book doesn't try to ignore the bad days or advocate a stiff upper lip. Far from it! It's vital to acknowledge your feelings, whatever they are and however scary they may be, at every stage of the process. Once you've recognized how you feel and allowed yourself to let those feelings out where necessary, you'll slowly start to find that the bad days are fewer than the good.

I'm not going to batter you with lots of touchy-feely gobbledegook either. Well, not all the time anyway! Divorce is not just about feelings; it's a very practical, very real issue that affects every aspect of your daily life. Many of the ideas here explore ways to equip you for dealing with the big questions of how to cope when divorce starts to eat away at your assets as well as your emotions.

There are practical ideas to help you decide what to do with your home and your possessions, as well as tips for dealing with thorny issues like telling your children and your parents. And there are also ideas that will ensure you dot all your legal i's and cross all your financial t's with the success of an attorney and the accuracy of an accountant.

You may have been told that divorce is like a bereavement, and you may be scared that you'll never get over it. But even if you do feel like this at first, it won't always be this bad. I'm not being trite, I promise! As I said, divorce, like bereavement, is a process. You will feel hurt, angry, sad, and betrayed (delete or add as applicable!). But there is no reason why you can't emerge from this process stronger and much more self-aware. At that stage you'll realize why I've added ideas on dating again and even remarriage.

I know from personal experience how tough things can be. I know how alone you can feel during a divorce, and I know that even when it's over you can still have days when you feel more wobbly than jelly. Divorced after ten years from a man I fully expected to spend the rest of my life with, there were days when I felt I had nothing more to look forward to than an evening in with the DVD sobbing over my old photos. I knew no one who'd been divorced and all my friends were buying big family homes, SUVs, and having babies. When I went out I felt I should wear black and sit quietly in case I upset anyone with my tales of woe.

None of my peers had gone through the same thing, and for the first time in my life I didn't have my husband to turn to for help and advice. So I started to look outside of my own frame of reference to discover ways to help myself. And you know it's just like when you learn to drive or get pregnant: You suddenly see student drivers and strollers everywhere! The young girl who ran my local dance class and turned it into a thriving business was chatting one day, and told me how she'd got divorced recently, too, and used the experience to fuel her independence. The older guy at the insurance brokers turned out to be twice divorced, married for the third time, and now ecstaticaly happy and full of encouraging advice.

The woman at the bank, who I'd always thought was a bit scary, was incredibly sympathetic when I went in to change my name on their records because she'd been through it, too. Even the most respectable woman in the bookshop turned out to have had an early divorce in her twenties before settling down with her cardigan-wearing, dictionary-reading second husband. I learned to view my parents as people and realized that their divorce after twenty-six years of marriage could teach me something, too.

The thing to realize is that even if you feel alone, you're not. So many people have been through and are going through it, too. Their finances have been burnt, their emotions fried, and their lives changed. But they have survived and the majority have gone on to much brighter futures.

This book turns the experiences of the people I've met, as well as my own, into 52 ways of not just surviving divorce, but coming out on the other side as a positive and powerful person. So take a deep breath and get reading!

1

Once upon a time . . .

. . . there lived a guy and a girl. They fell in love. He bought a ring. She said I do. Confetti rained down. The kids grew up. And they retired to the coast. But how often does this really happen? With about half of marriages breaking down, divorce is becoming a daily reality.

If the idea of "together forever" has lost its fairy-tale charm for you, this idea will help you take the first step toward divorce with pragmatism and without losing your hope for a happy ending. You're not alone.

MARRIAGE—FAIRY TALE OR NIGHTMARE?

Have you ever wondered why a fairy tale always ends with the wedding scene? Well, fairy tales are about weddings, not marriages. We get carried away on a cloud of tulle and think that the sweetness of the wedding cake will satisfy us forever. But sometimes it seems that our happily-ever-after vanishes with the last wedding guest.

Here's an idea for you . . .

Review your expectations. Although divorce is a powerful and useful tool, it has to be wielded carefully. You may need to end your marriage, but why not have a last reality check?

- **Are you expecting a perfect relationship?**
- **Do you expect never to argue?**
- **Do you always expect to be right?**
- **Do you always expect your own way?**
- **Do you expect not to have to work hard at your relationship?**

If you or your partner answers yes to more than two of these questions then perhaps you truly are expecting a fairy tale.

Weddings have always been common. The union between a man and a woman is primal, and our need to legitimize it is almost as old. Divorce, although an aged institution, has never been so common as it is today. But does that mean relationships in the past were always the happier ones? Not at all. It's just much more acceptable to be divorced now than it was then. For centuries, to be divorced was to be a social outcast. Of course, money and power in every age have provided notable exceptions but, even then, few people would look to Henry VIII as a role model for relationships.

The passing of time lessened the social stigma of divorce and it even became a tag of glamour in certain circles. For most, though, the breakdown of marriage is never glamorous, but it is a reality. In fact it's now rare to find someone who hasn't experienced divorce, either firsthand or through their parents or children.

So why has the stigma of divorce lessened? Well, society has changed. The role of women has changed: They're able to be financially independent in a way that was impossible in years gone by. One result of this is that they no longer have to stay in unhappy relationships for fear of losing every means of support they have. Another reason is that religion is less dominant these days and, therefore, the religious rules that once dominated society no longer have such power. It's notable that in Italy, Spain, Cyprus, and Greece, all deeply Catholic or Orthodox countries, the divorce rates are at their lowest.

Even princes and princesses can't live in a fairy tale. Look at IDEA 50, *The divorce hall of fame*, and see that divorce can happen to anyone.

Try another idea . . .

Of course, the decline of religion and the rise of feminism aren't the only reasons for the increase in divorce and the decrease of its stigma. Many other factors come into play, but a common theme is that both individuals and society are now less accepting of things they find unpleasant or unbearable, so if our marriages are broken beyond repair we no longer feel we have to limp through our lives without the hope of happiness with someone new. And that has to be a good thing.

UNLOCKING WEDLOCK WORLDWIDE

The number of couples divorcing worldwide is increasing year after year. In many countries, over one in two couples who've said "I do" are now saying "I don't." Belarus tops the table with a staggering 68 percent of marriages ending in divorce. The UK is close behind with 53 percent and here in the US, 49 percent of married couples go to the divorce courts each year.

So, should we start issuing divorce papers with every marriage certificate to save time? Well not every country is reporting a race toward marital meltdown. Italy reports only 12 percent of marriages ending in divorce, Cyprus 13 percent,

"Love does not begin and end the way we seem to think it does. Love is a battle, love is a war, love is a growing up."
JAMES BALDWIN, author

Defining idea . . .

Spain 17 percent, and Greece 18 percent. Maybe it's the Mediterranean climate or something they put in the olive oil, but the marriages in these sunny climes are far more likely to last the course than in many other countries.

What makes the difference? Why is divorce an epidemic in some countries and a rare disease in others? Will geography determine the success of your marriage, or are there any preventive measures short of moving to Tuscany that you can take? Of course it's hard to diagnose a blanket cause for the rise of divorce worldwide, but those common threads of religion and the role of women are woven through the statistics. It's important to realize, however, that numbers don't paint the whole picture and that marriage and divorce are always unique to the couple concerned.

How did it go?

Q   **Is there still a stigma attached to being a single parent?**

A   *As divorce becomes more common, so do single parents. Quite simply, the more single parents there are, the less acceptable it is for society to be critical of them.*

Q   **How can I avoid becoming just another statistic?**

A   *Communication, love, understanding, and tolerance are all key to making a relationship work. Sometimes, however, even these qualities can't make something right if it's wrong. Even if your marriage has failed, don't see yourself as a statistic but as an individual. Learn from the past and move on with your future.*

2

Maybe the va-va-voom can work for you

We all know that lust doesn't last, but passion can. Before you have a fling, try to put the zing back in your marriage. It can be done.

No one thinks it's strange that a middle-aged man is still as passionate about his football team as he was as a boy, or that a woman gets as excited as a girl every time she goes on a shopping spree. That's seen as normal. But feeling passionate about a long-term partner is viewed as unusual, something rare, and even a little strange. It doesn't have to be like that.

We almost expect not to experience passion in a marriage after a certain amount of time has passed; to think it's normal to be more interested in stroking the dog than each other. And if we expect something to happen, then it quite frequently does.

Here's an idea for you . . .

Send a text message saying "I love you and I miss holding you. I would be so happy if we could make love tonight, and I hope this makes you happy, too." Of course, it has to be in your own words and something you feel comfortable with, but the message should be open and simple. A sexy email or text can be just what you need to put the va-va-voom back in your relationship. It has the trademarks of dating and, therefore, associates all those feelings of excitement.

As long-term married couples, we are programed not to be passionate. That is often the reason why so many relationships go stale before their sell-by date. Of course, no one expects you to be lusting after each other like love-struck teenagers, but a marriage without sex can be unhealthy and destructive.

Television would have us all believe that sex is a romping, steamy roller coaster of a lovefest, best had between two beautiful people under the age of thirty. And if it isn't like that, well then it's probably best not to bother and to do some gardening instead. That's nonsense. Sex between real people can take many guises, and if you're on that roller coaster, then great! But if you're not, don't give up. A ride on the charming, slower, and slightly old-fashioned carousel can be just as enjoyable and far less stomach-churning than the big dipper. The secret is finding out what's good for both of you.

So, how do you do that? You've stopped making love, the cat sleeps closer to you than your partner, and you vaguely remember last having sex only after going overboard with the eggnog a few Christmases ago. Now you're talking about divorce. After all, the postman has started to look more appealing than your husband, especially the way his muscles ripple when he lifts his sack. And the woman at the supermarket handles the root vegetables in a way that makes you weak at the knees.

If your own partner feels as exciting as a trip to the supermarket, maybe now *is* the time to move on, cut your losses, and see if you can recapture the va-va-voom with someone new. But if you feel even the faintest tingle when you look at your partner, then it's worth trying one more trip to the fairground before you sign on the dotted line and finish it for good.

If you really can't face talking to each other, why not try getting a third party involved? Take a look at the tips in IDEA 21, *Stop hating, start communicating*, for where to start.

Try another idea . . .

LET'S TALK ABOUT SEX

Have you ever talked about sex with each other? Or was sex something that came so naturally to start with that there was no need to talk then, and now you don't know how to approach the subject? Well here's how to cope, even if you'd rather walk around Target naked than talk about sex with your partner—especially as talking about divorce seems an easier option.

Remember that easier isn't always better, and there are always alternative approaches to every problem. Just think about the number of ways we have to communicate today: phone, fax, email, text messaging, even the good old-fashioned letter. And it doesn't have to be complicated. Sometimes, especially if there has been a long gap since you last made love, long, involved explanations and accusations can just get in the way.

Good with words? Then what about the traditional romance of a letter? If not, then this is where the simplicity of an email or text message can really help. You may be thinking

"Sex is an emotion in motion."
MAE WEST

Defining idea . . .

this seems cold and shallow, but if you really can't talk about it face-to-face you need a catalyst to get the dialogue started. What have you got to lose? Once you're talking face-to-face, your ultimate goal of *doing* something else face-to-face is much more achievable.

Be brave—get talking before you start walking. Try having your discussion somewhere outside the bedroom. Remove the pressure from the situation. Open some wine, or take a walk together, but always make sure your partner feels safe, special, and loved.

How did it go?

Q   Why didn't it work? I sent my husband a sexy email at work and he was furious!

A   *He may work in an open plan office or share a computer screen and have been embarrassed if someone else saw it. Apologize, then leave it for a while and try to talk about it in a relaxed setting. Next time, think about when he'll receive it.*

Q   Why hasn't my wife written back? I told her I'm frustrated that we don't make love anymore, and I said maybe I would have to find someone new who does want sex.

A   *I'm not surprised she hasn't replied! Never threaten your partner or your relationship with infidelity. Try again and focus on her. Tell her you miss her and the intimacy that sex brings to your relationship. Tell her she's attractive and sexy. This will work a lot better.*

3

I told you so . . .

Are you trembling as you stand by the fireplace ready to tell the family? Worried about their reaction and a little scared? Concerned they'll disapprove or be unsupportive? Ditch the jitters and take control.

Feelings of apprehension are normal when you're about to tell your parents of a life change. But there's no point delaying—tell them now.

Life-changing events such as separation and divorce can make us feel very alone and scared. Our habitual patterns are being broken; the security that lies in the familiar has been destroyed, and we are moving into completely unknown territory. It's at moments like these that, if we are lucky enough still to have them in our lives, we feel the need for our parents.

Perfect parents will love their children unconditionally and will be a constant force of support and understanding throughout their childhoods and adult years. But, as we all know, very few relationships are perfect and that is as true for a parent/child relationship as it is for any other. Maybe you're lucky enough to have parents that will give you unconditional support as you go through your divorce, but if not, and you feel let down and upset by their response, it's worth remembering that although you feel it's *you* who should be at the center of everyone's thoughts, with

Here's an idea for you . . .

Prepare yourself in advance for the waterworks. What will you do? It can be very upsetting to see your parents cry, and you don't want to end up running away calling for your grandparents. Be prepared for this reaction before you tell them so if they do become tearful you'll be far more likely to be able to cope. (And, if they don't, you'll be pleasantly surprised.) Give them some time to recover, make a cup of tea, and, if you have that sort of relationship, give them a hug.

your needs coming first at this time, your parents will have their own feelings to deal with, too. They may well need some time to adjust to the changes and stresses that your divorce will mean for them. This is especially true if you have children.

So, how do you tell them? Being straightforward and honest about the situation is definitely the best choice. You may feel you want to hide it from them to spare their feelings, but divorce is a final separation between you and your spouse, and it is better to be up front about the situation from the start. Never think that other people cannot cope with the realities of your life.

BITE THE BULLET

OK, so it's time to break the bad news and you want to do it without quivering, quaking, and sucking your thumb. But how do you cope with the face-to-face encounter? Mental rehearsal is key. You've probably got a reasonably good idea as to what their reaction will be. If your mom and your wife happily baked brownies together every Saturday, or your husband and father spent every home game at Giants Stadium together munching on hotdogs, then they're probably not going to be thrilled with your news.

Imagine what the worst reaction will be and plan some responses. Explain that, although you know they were very close to your partner, the intimacy between the two of you as husband and wife is no longer there. Long and rambling explanations will get you nowhere. So be simple, calm, and to the point when explaining the situation or responding to their questions. Deep breathing and staying focused on a clear idea of your aims and objectives in the conversation should help you to stay in control.

If you start to get cross, use the anger management techniques talked about in IDEA 19, *Are you speaking my language?* They'll help you make sure you don't start throwing things.

Try another idea . . .

Maybe they'll pour on the drama and say that losing their son/daughter-in-law is like losing a child. If you feel comfortable with your parents continuing a relationship with your ex then tell them so. If not, firmly state that the situation is very painful for you, too, and reassure them that *you* will always be their child no matter what your marital status is.

So what happens if, even after you've told them the news as calmly as you can, your mother or even father breaks down in tears that threaten to drown the dog? Don't panic! This is where the mental rehearsal comes in.

But have you thought that their reactions might be completely different from the one you expected? Maybe your parents always warned you against the evils of being with your spouse and feel their views are coming home to

"Children sweeten labors but they make misfortunes more bitter."
FRANCIS BACON

Defining idea . . .

roost. At least they'll be on your side, but you must also be wary of getting sucked into a negative pattern of demonizing your ex.

Your parents aren't perfect and they will have their own views and opinions of your divorce. You must stay strong, focus on your needs, and remember . . . if you're old enough to marry and divorce, you're old enough to cope with your mom and dad.

How did it go?

Q **I was prepared for the initial upset, but how can I help my mother stop crying every time she sees me?**

A *You can't. What you can do is say that her crying upsets you and hope this has an effect. If not, just remember that her reactions are her responsibility . . . and buy a box of tissues.*

Q **I explained the situation as best as I could to my dad, so how come he still blames me for the divorce?**

A *Put the question to him. Tell him you're confused by his response and ask him to explain why he blames you. If you're too angry or upset to do so, ask your mom or a sibling to talk to him on your behalf.*

4

Online is divine

The divorce is over, you've done your grieving or your celebrating, and now you're ready to give the dating scene a try again. The web is a great place to meet someone new and have some fun. You might even fall in love.

Where on earth do you start? When you're trying to build a new life, you can use the latest technology available to make your return to dating as painless as possible.

LOG ON FOR LOVE

Getting back into the dating game can be daunting after a divorce. Of course, some people are so eager to get back onto the horse of love that the ink is hardly dry on the papers before they're propping up the bar at their local singles club. But for those of us who rate a trip to a singles bar as about as much fun as a trip to the dentist, then online really can be divine.

Consider this: unless you fancy heading off to a speed-dating event, where else can you sift through thirty prospective dates in an evening? Or where can you state your exact requirements for a new partner up front without being considered pushy?

Be clear about your requirements for a possible partner and draw up a list. Don't be shy of stating that you want a smoker or someone keen on fitness and vegetarianism. This can avoid a lot of time wasted on people who just aren't right for you. When filtering through your responses, focus on the things that appeal to you. If she's into salsa dancing, eating out, and books by John Updike, just like you, but can't punctuate, then ignore the grammar and grab the girl!

Online dating is a gift from the cyber gods for those of us who have gone through a divorce. The chances are that we'll be very wary of making the same mistakes again—meeting the same kind of partner from hell or falling for yet another pair of twinkling, yet wandering, eyes. Arranging dates online gives us an enlightened perspective and a chance to filter out a good proportion of the love rats and liars without ever having to meet them. All you need to do is gain access to the Internet, write a personal profile, follow a few easy guidelines, and you could be canoodling in the back row of the theater by Friday.

As with all things, your personal safety must come first. Although the Internet has developed a bit of a bad reputation where personal interactions are concerned, it's only a few bad apples that have soured the cider. If you stick to reputable websites there's no reason why online dating should pose any extra threats. In fact, it can be safer to meet new people online than it is to go down to your local nightclub and meet them there.

Use personal recommendations for dating sites and always check the privacy policy. A legitimate site will guarantee not to share your personal information with any other party. It will also ensure that all correspondence is made anonymously through the site until you're ready to exchange private emails.

CYBER-CUPID

Did you know that Date.com, an Internet dating firm, has claimed that their site leads to one marriage every week? Well, even if your intentions aren't quite so serious, it's still easy to meet your e-match from heaven on the net.

Is your divorce taking so long that your next date will be in the old folks home? Check out IDEA 14, *Dating dilemmas*, for the pros and cons of dating before the divorce is final.

Try another idea . . .

First of all, create a catchy online name for yourself that is positive and fun. Rather than calling yourself "Lonely but Lovely" go for "Full of Fun," for instance. Keep your details short and sweet, but leave out any shortcomings you feel you have. Start with a flattering physical description in the first line and include a good photo. Statistics show that you're eight times more likely to receive a response with a photo than without, and even a bad one is better than nothing.

Include specifics—your favorite film, what music and hobbies you're into. Add some of your ambitions so you come across as a person with goals and a positive future, but don't say something like "I'm desperate to become a father by next Christmas!" unless you want your inbox to remain empty.

Once you've spotted your possible date, it's time to start up an email relationship. Most sites will allow you to browse their lists for free and even post a profile. But if you want to respond to someone, that's when the charges will kick in. After emailing for a bit, move on to chatting on the phone. If and when you feel comfortable, arrange a date and wait for Cupid's arrow to strike!

"Don't be afraid to take a big step. You can't cross a chasm in two small jumps."
DAVID LLOYD GEORGE

Defining idea . . .

When going on a date, tell someone where you're going, even if you're a guy, and arrange to meet a friend afterward. Meet in a busy public place, and remember, always trust your instincts—if you're getting bad vibes, leave.

How did it go?

Q   I'd like to give it a try, but I'm worried. Isn't it just weirdos and nerds on the Internet?

A   *Definitely not! There are loads of people just like you. You could try a specialist site to ensure you are with like-minded people, or browse through a number of regular sites. You'll be surprised how many ordinary people use the Internet to get a date.*

Q   Why haven't I had any responses? My details have been posted for weeks.

A   *The answer probably lies with your profile. Get a friend to read it and give you some feedback. Maybe you're being negative? If you've got something like "I'm a size sixteen and constantly dieting," change it to "I'm a gorgeous girl with an hourglass figure who loves dining out." It's all in the spin!*

5
Circle of friends

This idea helps you understand why your circle of married friends is ever diminishing as soon as you first mention the word "divorce." And it helps you make new chums, too.

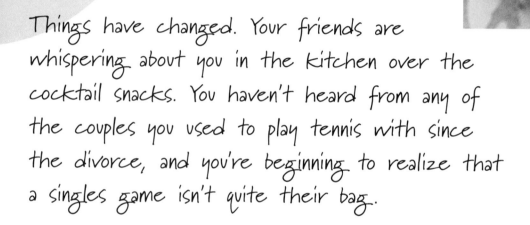

Things have changed. Your friends are whispering about you in the kitchen over the cocktail snacks. You haven't heard from any of the couples you used to play tennis with since the divorce, and you're beginning to realize that a singles game isn't quite their bag.

ARE YOUR FRIENDS A BAND OF GOLD, OR A BAND ON THE RUN?

When you get divorced, you suddenly realize that you've become a "one" and suddenly life seems very unfair on the odd numbers.

It's hard the first time you realize that many of your friends are adopting the "sieve and sand" approach to friendship—one little shake-up and they've all disappeared.

Here's an idea for you . . .

It's time to put yourself first. Divorce is a time when you need real support from people around you. However, many people feel isolated and alone during their divorce, so if you're not getting the support you need from your friends then look at other alternatives. Families can be great, as can taking up new hobbies to broaden your circle of acquaintances. If you still haven't got someone to talk to who understands exactly how you feel, check out a support group. There are lots of groups around for people going through divorce, as well as for single parents. Look online or at your local library and you'll soon see that you don't need to go through this alone.

But, although it may seem difficult at first, it's much better to find out who your real friends are right from the start.

Of course you need to work hard at your existing friendships. Things have changed for you and that will change the balance of your relationship with your friends. Be honest with them about how you feel. Tell them if you need their support or if you need some time alone. Don't ignore them, and listen to their views, too. However, don't feel bad if your friends turn out to be as supportive as shot underwear elastic.

Even if you have been friends with people for years, your change of status from married to single will necessitate some adjustment on their part. Many couples, even if they're usually as together as peaches and cream, will see your new single status as a threat to their own stability. If this is the case, be flattered! When you were comfortably cocooned in marriage your friends may have never noticed you as a sexual being. But now perhaps they do. So even if you wouldn't go near your ugly friend Terry after a gallon of tequila, Terry's wife may think you will. Instead of getting upset and emphasizing Terry's more repellent qualities, take it as a compliment. You're back to being single and sexy and people are noticing.

Maybe you've got too many friends with too many opinions and your circle of friends is starting to strangle you. Take a look at IDEA 22, *Don't do it like that—do it like this!*, and get some breathing space.

Try another idea . . .

Now is the time to put yourself first, so focus on friends who can see *you* and not just their own insecurities. If you find you're a bit short of such people, actively try to widen your social circle.

"Good idea, but how?" you might ask. Well, think of any interest you may have and go for it, however boring or wild that may be. There's no one to stop you now. Research it on the Internet or through the library and find out about any ways you can get involved.

Whatever interesting activities you fancy, cast out the fishing line of friendship and see what bites you get. Obviously, it will take a while to develop a circle of friends as good as the ones on *Friends*, especially as you're going through a big change in your life, so be patient. And even if you find yourself sitting on your mom's sofa eating Pop Tarts for the third time this week instead of drinking Americano at Central Perk, don't panic! Just make sure that tomorrow you're trying something new.

"A true friend is like a good bra: It's hard to find, lifts you up when you're down, gives you support, and is always close to your heart."
ANONYMOUS

Defining idea . . .

How did
it go?

Q **Is it too late to make new friends? I'm fifty-nine and recently divorced.**

A *Never! More and more people are divorcing in their fifties and sixties so there are lots of people out there in your position. Go to the local library and see if there are any evenings for divorced people in your area. If this doesn't appeal, try a new hobby or resurrect an old one that will bring you into contact with new people. Also remember that people don't have to be exactly the same age or background as you to become your friends.*

Q **Why has my best friend had a bad reaction to my divorce? She hardly speaks to me and now spends our regular Tuesday night out with her husband.**

A *Maybe she feels that now that you're single you'll find new friends, and she is protecting herself. In some ways she may see your life-change as exciting, while hers remains the same. Tell her how you feel—that you need her now more than ever and make a firm plan for next Tuesday night.*

6

DIY divorce

**With divorce rates rising every year, the attorneys' pockets
are bulging, and many people find the expense of divorce
a shock and a struggle. There is a way to keep the cash in
your own pockets—simply do the divorce yourself.**

Will a DIY divorce save you money, or just
store up trouble? If you'd like to cut costs, but
don't want a DIY disaster, then here's some
advice that won't cost you a fortune.

Given that attorneys' charges can range from $200 per hour plus costs to the upper
echelons of the financial stratosphere, it's worth considering taking the DIY route to
divorce and preventing your finances from getting hammered in the process. If you
think your ex-to-be is likely to make the divorce procedure stickier than superglue,
then get an attorney and save yourself from the DIY divorce casualty ward.
However, if you and your spouse have decided to part as painlessly as possible, then
doing it yourselves will save you a fortune.

You may wonder how easy it really is to do the legwork of the divorce yourselves.
Well, as long as there are no disputes or complexities with property and assets, it

Here's an idea for you . . .

Get divorced online! There are lots of Internet services offered to help you get divorced. Many have a fixed-price guarantee and can be a much cheaper way of untying the knot than using an attorney. Be careful, though, and check everything out thoroughly before parting with any cash. There are also a number of services available where you can ask online attorneys your legal questions rather than visiting them in person. Personal recommendations are the best way to find a good service. If you become worried at any stage, get the professionals in and hire an attorney in the regular way.

can be quite straightforward. You will need to be up to scratch in terms of literacy and bureaucracy to understand the various forms that have to be completed, but other than that there are no real obstacles. There's also a lot of free advice you can find in the library or online, and a local bookshop may also offer guidance books.

TOOLS OF THE TRADE

First, it is important to remember that divorce laws vary from state to state. You'll want to purchase a state-specific guide or book to walk you through the particulars. Or, if you're computer-savvy, there are several DIY divorce software packages available.

Generally, the process will begin with you filling out your petition for divorce. This document lists all the pertinent details—the names of you and your spouse, the reason for your divorce (in amicable situations like this, the standard no-fault grounds are "irreconcilable differences"), and the stipulations you'd like to set forth for the dissolution of your marriage. You then file the petition with the court.

Your spouse must be officially notified when the petition has been filed. You can opt to pay the court to serve your soon-to-be ex with notification papers or simply deliver them yourself.

Take a look at IDEA 43, Attorneys—saints or sinners? if DIY law isn't for you.

Try another idea . . .

Upon receipt of notification, your spouse can elect to sign a waiver, which indicates to the court that he accepts the terms of the petition and offers no challenges. This will eliminate any need for him to appear in court, if he chooses.

If the court accepts your petition, you enter a mandatory waiting period (these vary by state and can be anywhere from ninety days to six months) during which you make certain you want to go through with the divorce. If children are involved, the court will hold a hearing to establish temporary custody and alimony details.

During the waiting period, you and your spouse will iron out the specifics of the divorce agreement, including division of assets, custody and visitation rights, alimony, and any other particulars. These decisions will make up your final decree of divorce.

"Divorce is a declaration of independence with only two signers."
GERALD F. LIEBERMAN, writer and philosophical thinker

Defining idea . . .

When time's up on the waiting period, you can schedule a court date. On that day, put on your Sunday best, bring all the necessary paperwork, and present yourself to the judge. You will read the document you and your spouse put together, and if the judge is satisfied that the agreement is fair and lawful, he will grant the divorce on the spot.

As soon as your paperwork is stamped, you will know that your DIY divorce has been successful. You can now remarry, run off to Reykjavik, or simply throw a party!

How did it go?

Q **Can I represent myself in court?**

A *In some cases you can. However, I would advise against it. It may seem like a good way to save cash, but you could lose out in the long term if your ex-to-be is using a professionally trained legal team.*

7

Take a walk on the child's side

Don't let your kids feel your function after divorce is little more than providing a McDonald's Happy Meal and a Sunday trip to the zoo. See things from a pint-size point of view.

The term "weekend parent" is one we are becoming all too familiar with and one rife with negative connotations. But with more and more children experiencing the divorce of their parents, there has to be a way to soothe the sting of separation for our children.

THE CHILD HAS TO WIN

There's no reason that a "weekend parent" has to become a "weakened parent." Just because the bond between you and your partner as husband and wife has been broken, it doesn't necessarily mean the bond between you and your child will break as well.

Here's an idea for you . . .

Make sure that your child knows he will always see the parent who is leaving on a regular basis. That may be every weekend or every day, but make sure, for the first few months at least, this doesn't change. Even if your child has unlimited access to you or your ex, it's still important to keep a routine involved.

If divorce is inevitable, be honest with your kids. A friend of mine was terrified about telling her children about the divorce. She put it off for weeks until she had to attend court and couldn't hide the facts any longer. When she finally sat down to tell her ten- and thirteen-year-old, the last thing she expected was for her children to look solemnly at her and say, "Dad moved out weeks ago, so we knew you were getting divorced. It happens all the time at school. But Mom, it would have been better if you told us so we didn't have to guess." Children are not stupid and deserve the truth. Telling them simply and reassuring them of your love will remove any unnecessary fears of the unknown.

Children are remarkably flexible and their love can stretch to encompass many a bizarre family situation. I have a friend whose child has three dads. "Bio-Dad" (his biological parent), "Ben-Dad" (his mother's first husband), and "My-Dad" (her second husband, who has formally adopted him). My friend's son is now a well-adjusted seventeen-year-old. In his words, "I know my family's a bit weird, but then being normal can be a bit boring. In my opinion I'm lucky to have three dads. It's a lot better than having no dad at all."

Of course children are always emotionally and practically affected by divorce, and there is never a "good" or "bad" age for your child to go through it. In fact, more psychological damage can be caused by the "staying for the kids" approach. The family atmosphere can become bitter and stale, arguments can become the staple of communication, and the child can ultimately feel to blame.

But divorce at any age will challenge your child's sense of stability and security and it's important to reassert some form of normality. A good way to do this is to quickly instigate a routine, as this will give a reliable pattern to your child's life. Knowing that they always have math on Monday morning at school might not be much fun, but it is a reality that doesn't change. And with that reality comes stability and a sense of place.

For more on understanding the emotional conflict at any age, see IDEA 31, *You can't get divorced, you're my parents!*

Try another idea . . .

Repetition is also a handy tool for creating stability. Your child needs to learn about the new way the family will work, and repetition is a key tool for effective learning. Constantly repeating yourself may require a lot of patience, especially at a time that's obviously very difficult for you, but it will pay off in the end. You may have to repeat the same answers to the same questions until you want to scream, but it will reassure and comfort your child. For instance, questions such as "Why did you have to leave Dad?" may need to be answered hundreds of times before it makes sense to your child. Repetition of words and actions forms the basis of all reassurance and routine and is essential in repairing any damage done by divorce.

The key is to be constantly aware of your child's state of mind and behavioral patterns. Notify your child's school and discuss the situation with the parents of your child's best friend. The up side of rising divorce statistics means it's likely that your child will have a friend at school who has gone through the same thing. Teachers are aware of the traumas a child of divorce will face and can respond accordingly; many schools also have

"The most important thing a father can do for his children is love their mother."
CONTEMPORARY TRUISM

Defining idea . . .

on-site counselors for emotional support. Your child will need a support network in a similar way that you will. Friends, family, and teachers can all help to provide stability and support at a time when you may find it difficult to do so.

Divorce is never going to be easy for any family, but with the implementation of some practical ideas, it can become a rite of passage for your child rather than simply a passage to depression and despair.

How did it go?

Q   How can I convince my child that the divorce is not her fault?

A   *This is a normal response from a child. It's her way of making sense of the situation. You need to provide her with another way to do this. Explain honestly about what caused your marriage breakup. If possible, enlist the help of your ex to reassure your child that she was not to blame.*

Q   How can I stop my son from telling everyone that his father and I will eventually get back together?

A   *Explain again to him that a divorce is final. It means that you and your ex are separated by law and will not live together again. Check that your ex isn't giving your son another version of the story. If he is saying the same as you and your son still has a problem accepting the separation, then it may be a good idea for him to talk to a counselor.*

8

Boiling point on the sea of love

Affairs? Betrayal? Boredom? You've reached the boiling point. Maybe it's a slow move toward separation, or a complete shock that your marriage is bubbling over. Take a look at precisely why your marriage might be melting.

We all claim we know that marriage won't always be easy. But are we ever really prepared for some of the storms that we'll encounter on the sea of love? Probably not.

SAILING THE STORMY SEA OF LOVE

When we say we'll be together no matter what, we tend to be in the first bloom of love, or at the very start of our married lives together. We feel that our love is strong enough to weather any storm and we'll work through any situation together.

But every boat, from a little dinghy to a supertanker, needs constant maintenance, fuel, and care to save it from sinking, as well as realistic expectations about its durability. Even the most beautiful, powerful, unsinkable cruise ship in the world

Here's an idea for you . . .

If you've found out that your spouse wants a divorce and you're in shock, it's time for some damage control. You must limit the distress before it causes you any irreparable damage. First off, allow yourself to cry and shout out the worst feelings of pain and betrayal; don't try to keep them inside. Then call someone, a friend or family member, to come and sit with you. Arrange time off work to cope with your shock privately and to organize any practicalities. Let your work know it's a personal crisis and if you have children, inform their school. Most important, take some time to come to terms with the news before you jump to any hasty decisions. Think things through carefully and talk any plans through with someone you trust.

went down after its first bump, didn't it? Maybe suggesting the iceberg that sank the *Titanic* was a bit of a bump is a slight understatement, but you get the point. Awareness, forethought, and constant monitoring of what's up ahead is key to saving your marriage from following the *Titanic* down into the depths.

Many people have asked, "What if the ship's designers hadn't been so cocky about the unsinkable nature of their ship? What if they'd placed more lifeboats on board? What if they'd had a better lookout system than a tiny man in a little crow's nest in a lot of fog?" But then life is full of "what-ifs?", and the same is true of marriage. If you are considering divorce, then the reality is that your marriage is sailing very precariously on a stormy sea. It's time to check if you can stop it from sinking before you swim solo for the shore.

BUBBLING OVER

So, is it possible to bring certain situations down to a gentle simmer before they boil over? Well, it depends what has brought things to the point of breakup and whether you have the desire to fix the damage or not.

The most common cause of a relationship coming to an instant crisis point is infidelity. Is it even possible to save the marriage if you've been unfaithful and your spouse has found out? Well, the first thing to do is ask yourself the questions: why did you do it and was it a one-time fling or a full-blown affair? Be honest with yourself. Once you've discovered the reasons behind your infidelity, you may well discover underlying problems, which you either want to fix, or you don't.

An affair is possibly the major cause of marital breakup. It contravenes the basic premise of marriage—sexual fidelity. Once the affair is discovered, the bond of trust between husband and wife is severely damaged. However, an affair needn't mean that the marriage is doomed. It will take a great deal of courage and commitment to work through the hurt and distrust that is the legacy of infidelity, but it can be done if both partners want it enough.

Boiling points in relationships can also come out of situations that are far less dramatic, but equally destructive. Perhaps you're just bored. It's common to become bored with your spouse, your house, your life—suddenly you want some excitement, some passion. You want a divorce! But is this really about your spouse's shortcomings, or is it about you?

Your marriage doesn't have to die through boredom. Take a look at IDEA 2, *Maybe the va-va-voom can work for you*, and see if you can make each other boil with passion instead of irritation.

Try another idea . . .

"Divorce is probably of nearly the same date as marriage. I believe however that marriage is some weeks the more ancient."
VOLTAIRE

Defining idea . . .

31

Maybe if you were to change yourself first, to find some new challenges and ease the boredom, you might begin to feel differently about your partner. Talk about the situation, state how you feel, and see if there's any way you can get what you crave and stay within your marriage. Understanding of the deeper reasons behind these issues can be vital if you want to change your course from due north to divorce.

How did it go?

Q **How can I forgive my husband? He had an affair with my best friend.**

A *Only you can decide if you can forgive him. Give yourself time to get over the shock. After all, you've been betrayed by your friend as well as your husband. Once the dust has settled, ask yourself these questions: Do you still love him? Can you trust him again? Is he sorry and eager to move on with your marriage? The answers should give you some guidance.*

Q **Should I leave my husband? I can't stand him anymore! He irritates me intensely, and I can hardly bear to hold a conversation with him!**

A *You've obviously reached the boiling point in your marriage, but that doesn't have to be the end. Ask yourself why your husband makes you feel this way. Is there a deeper problem behind your irritation? If there is, are you committed enough to your marriage to find out and work it through? If so, you've answered your own question.*

9

Give yourself the power to let go

It's over. You've signed the forms, you've reached a settlement, and you've finished arguing over the possessions. But you're still taking deep breaths rather than breathing a sigh of relief. Here's how you can let go and finally feel free.

Some things we can change. Some things we can fix. Some things we just have to let go. This is especially true of divorce. Your marriage is something that couldn't be changed and couldn't be fixed; so now you need to let it go.

COLD TURKEY ISN'T JUST IN YOUR SANDWICHES

Other people may think this is the easy bit. After all, you've survived the divorce proceedings, haven't you? Well, yes you have, and congratulations! You know you've done well, you know you've been strong and seen it through, so why can't you put it behind you and move on?

33

Here's an idea for you . . .

If you're finding it hard to let go, then list your ex's Top Ten Faults. Write down all those habits that drove you crazy. List all the negative points and forget about the good things for a while. When you've got your ultimate list of nasties, rip the list into tiny pieces and hurl them in the trash. Doing this banishes the need to hang on to your marriage and really gets you to let go. Go on—I promise you'll feel better!

We are all creatures of routine and habit. We go to work every day, we have television programs we always watch and regular hobbies. We also have bad habits that we find addictive and very hard to break such as smoking and drinking. Your marriage was in a way a routine. You were probably in it for a long time, and you got used to being there. Bad marriages can become bad habits. Even if they make us unhappy or ill, we can still find them an addictive routine that's hard to kick. So that's why you're finding it hard to let go.

Your marriage was something that defined you, and now it's gone. Eventually you will form new routines with other people and for yourself, but you need to unlearn the old ones first. The trick is to stop yourself from going cold turkey and to let your marriage go gently. Don't expect to get over your divorce overnight, but start to make a positive choice to place your focus elsewhere. It's time to give up your old bad habits so you've got plenty of room for new ones.

RELEASE YOUR GRIP

It's really important to loosen your grip on the past. It's time to accept your divorce and the fact that your one-time partner is now your ex. Focus on staying strong, and before you know it you'll be flying toward your future rather than being stuck with the bad habits of your past.

Start by letting your feelings out. If this means shouting and screaming, then do so. Just find yourself a private place where you won't be overheard and give it a lungful! If you're angry, invest in a punching bag, or grab a pillow, and thump it out of your system.

You're divorced and you've let go, but do you feel you need a little time to heal? Then take a look at IDEA 10, *Sore, raw, and single*, for advice on how to lick your wounds without wallowing.

Try another idea . . .

Unlocking your emotions may also unlock your grief. Don't worry about this or feel you're being weak. If you feel sad, acknowledge it and give yourself permission to grieve for your marriage. This is especially important if you are the one who has been left by your partner. Sit down with some old photos, either alone or with a friend, and reminisce. Allow yourself to mourn for what you have lost and cry if you need to. But afterward it's time to dry your eyes, look to the future, and move on.

Write a list of all the things you've learned from going through your divorce. Focus on how it's made you a stronger and wiser person. Congratulate yourself on surviving a difficult time and see it as an achievement. Recognize yourself as a survivor, someone who refuses to move backward, and feel proud that you saw it through. Then sit down and make a list of all the things you found unacceptable in your old relationship, and all the things you would look for in a new one.

"The secret of health for both body and mind is not to mourn for the past, worry about the future but to live in the present moment wisely and earnestly."
BUDDHA

Defining idea . . .

If you're missing something warm to cuddle at night, why not get a pet? A dog or a cat can provide companionship and unconditional love, which is more than you can say about your ex. In addition, having a pet in your life means you need to care for something other than yourself, which is an invaluable motivator.

How did it go?

Q   How can I stop dreaming about my ex-husband?

A   *You need to place some alternative images in your head before you go to sleep. Just before you doze off, visualize something in your life you'd really like to achieve. Maybe you want a sports car or a luxurious beach vacation. Find a picture if you can, and look at it, too. Relaxation tapes can help you focus firmly on your positive future goals.*

Q   How can I stop looking at my wedding photographs?

A   *Take a final look at them. Cry if you want to. Then package them up safely and give them to a trusted family member or friend to keep. That way you won't be tempted to get them out whenever you feel down, but you will know they are safe and you can have them back when you feel stronger.*

10

Sore, raw, and single

Worried you'll end up forever microwaving meals for one, boring your friends about the evils of the single supplement, and dancing around your living room to Gloria Gaynor's "I Will Survive" (even if you're a guy)? Then read this idea.

It's okay to feel battered; that's normal. Divorce is a hard road to travel. There are so many bumps and thumps along the way that we always emerge a little bruised when we reach our final destination.

DIVORCE DRIVE

Some of us navigate the road to divorce in a tiny, battered Volkswagen prone to breaking down and running out of fuel. However, using a bit of initiative, you can build a four-wheel drive off-roader that is armored and reliable. However, even the best protected car is liable to accidents, especially on a road as fraught with obstacles and unforeseen hazards as Divorce Drive. As a result we're all going to end up with a bruise or a sore patch somewhere by the end of the trip.

Avoid socializing again before you're ready. Tell your friends that you're not ready to get out there yet, but that after some healing time you will be. Remember to be friendly and polite when you decline invitations, but be firm. Set a time limit for licking your wounds and stick to it. When you tell your friends that you might not be up to the cocktail bar yet, arrange a firm date in a month's or six weeks' time when you will try it out. Suggest alternative ideas so that your friends won't feel alienated—perhaps a quiet meal out, or a video and takeout would work well.

The first thing to recognize, even if you are feeling a bit battered, is that you've survived the journey. So what if you've picked up some damage along the way? Show me someone who's managed to get through the journey of their life unscathed and I'll show you a very boring person!

We all know that life is a journey with many paths to follow and diversions to navigate. Divorce Drive is just one of these. If you're sensible it will be a one-way street that you'll have no desire to go down again. If you're still on Divorce Drive, the thing to remember is that divorce is a road with a finite length and it has a final destination—your freedom.

So, you've reached the end of the road, but now that you've got there you're sore, raw, and single. You may not even be that happy about being single. Is everyone going on about how great it is to be single and you're just too unhappy to appreciate it? Do you just want to wallow, lick your wounds, and recover? Sound familiar?

Remember that it is okay to wallow. Yes, that's right, you read that last bit correctly! It's perfectly acceptable to take some time out to recover from what you've been through. In fact it's a healthy approach to acknowledge your feelings of sadness and to give yourself some time to heal. And it's much better to allow yourself to get over the trauma of divorce before diving back into the world of relationships again.

> **Maybe however much healing time you have, you're still not moving forward with your life. Take a look at IDEA 38, *Moving on*, for some positive advice.**

Try another idea . . .

So, in order to ensure that you heal well, allow yourself to go through the process of recovery at your own speed. Start by acknowledging to yourself that you've been through a tough time. Don't try to put a brave face on it. Sit down, count your bruises, and cry if they hurt. Showing your bruises rather than covering them up is the first step to helping them heal.

Second, acknowledge to others that things have been tough for you and that you feel sore and raw at the moment. Don't feel you always have to face things alone. Choose one or two close friends or family members to share your feelings with and have a cry if you need to. Ask them to give you the opportunity and space to do this, but afterward get them to focus on something positive that has come from the divorce.

Giving yourself permission to be sad, taking some time to be alone and reflect, and acknowledging the pain you've been through will provide a good base from which to move forward. You are sore, you are raw, you are single. Understanding your feelings and giving yourself some time to heal today will ensure that you start to feel better tomorrow.

> *"You, yourself as much as anyone in the entire universe, deserve your love and affection."*
> BUDDHA

Defining idea . . .

39

Q **How do I stop poking at my bruises from the divorce? I know I need to move on, but haven't managed it yet.**

A *Remember, be kind to yourself. If you've had a night when you've been miserable, or eaten your body weight in chocolate, don't panic. So what if you've had a bad day? Don't beat yourself up about it. Simply commit to having a good day tomorrow. Think of something healthy and positive to do. Bike to work, see a film, or paint your bedroom.*

Q **How do I know how much time I should set before I socialize again?**

A *That depends on how sore and raw you feel. If your divorce has been very painful, you may need a little more time. Or you may feel after a few weeks you want to get out there again. Be flexible. Talk to your friends and the people who know you best. Make your own suggestion, say six weeks, and see how they respond to that.*

11

Breaking up needn't be hard to do

You've reached your decision and you want to break up. So, how are you going to do it? This idea takes you through the practicalities and helps you leave without breaking the wedding crystal or your heart.

For some of us the marital breakup comes with all the force of a hurricane. It sweeps through, leaving a trail of devastation and an eerie silence in its wake. This is particularly true if your partner has left out of the blue, but if this hasn't happened yet, a breakup can be handled without causing complete devastation.

FORECAST AND FOREARM

Hurricanes, although they begin seemingly out of nowhere, can usually be predicted. Meteorologists track barometric pressure, plot patterns of weather

Here's an idea for you . . .

If you know divorce is inevitable, have a breakup rehearsal. A friend of mine wanted to divorce her husband but always let him talk her out of it whenever she tried to tell him. She spent three extra years in an unhappy marriage until she realized she had to *plan and rehearse* her breakup in advance. First of all, she booked a hotel to go to directly after telling her husband. That way she had somewhere to stay even if he wouldn't leave the house himself. She then rehearsed exactly what she was going to say and wrote down prompts to use if she got nervous. She actively prepared herself for her husband's reactions so they didn't come as a surprise and throw her off balance. Finally she used deep breathing exercises to cope with her nervousness and to help her not to cry. Breaking up really is hard to do but if you follow my friend's advice it will most certainly be easier.

behavior, record dips or sudden rises in temperature, and forecast when and where the next one will strike. Nine times out of ten, they get it right. Prediction of marital breakups can be much the same. If you know what to look for, then you, too, can forecast the future. So, be your own relationship forecaster and track the pressure increases between you, plot patterns of behavior, and record the frequency of sudden dips in temperature in your marriage.

Of course, you will need to take a step outside the situation and look at things with a dispassionate perspective, but if you can take this view, you may well be able to predict if and when the breakup will come.

Forewarned and forecasted, as they say, is forearmed. A weather forecast gives residents in a hurricane zone the chance to batten down the hatches, make survival plans, and bolster up stores or defenses. You can do this, too. If you have some idea in advance that your spouse may be planning a split with you, then you can make some plans and get yourself emotionally and practically ready. And if you know it's coming anyway, why not jump in there first and break up on your terms?

A CLEAN BREAK

Now that you've managed a clean break, check out IDEA 28, *Dividing the spoils*, to make sure you split your possessions without breaking them, too.

Try another idea . . .

So, you know the breakup's coming; what next? The first thing to do is keep the sense of panic to a minimum and to prepare yourself. Do this by making positive choices about how you will deal with the situation. If it's you who wants the divorce, plan when and how you're going to tell your spouse. Avoid doing it spontaneously in the middle of an argument, or the middle of ShopRite. Instead make a time when you know you will have some space, and make sure the children are out of earshot. If you think your spouse plans to break up with you, mentally rehearse how you will deal with it and brace yourself for the inevitable emotional impact.

Also, have an idea of what you'll do immediately after the event. Perhaps you could tell a friend what you're planning to do, or what you think might happen and have her on standby for emotional or practical support. Prepare a number of options so you can fit them around how you're feeling. You may just want to go for a walk on your own, or you may just want to phone your mom.

Think about the practicalities involved well in advance. For example, you've both been living in the same house, and you're the one asking for the divorce. Does that mean you'll be the

"Nowadays love is a matter of chance, matrimony a matter of money, and divorce a matter of course."
HELEN ROWLAND, journalist

Defining idea . . .

one to leave? If so, arrange somewhere to stay while you sort things out. Work out how this will affect your children. You need to keep the practical disruption for them to a minimum, so ensure that some of their normal routines remain in place. Going to school and regular contact with their friends is essential.

How did it go?

Q **How do I tell my wife I want a divorce when we've just celebrated our tenth wedding anniversary?**

A *If you really want a divorce then you cannot afford to be sentimental. If the marriage is over then your wife has a right to know. Be clear and calm. Mentally rehearse what you have to say and how you will deal with her reaction.*

Q **How can I ask my husband to leave the marital home when he pays the mortgage and I stay at home to look after the children?**

A *Before you say anything to your husband, get some legal advice. Check out where you stand and exactly what your rights are. Don't threaten him with anything that won't stand up in a court of law.*

12

Marriage on trial

Before you head off to court for a divorce, maybe it's worth putting your marriage on trial one last time. Trial separation can sometimes provide the space you need to breathe, or seal the fate of your relationship. Let's look at the realities of a temporary split and see if it's right for you.

Whether we like it or not, it's a fact that trial separations are a gamble. But let's face it, if your marriage has gotten to that stage, then what have you got to lose?

KILL OR CURE

Popular belief holds that a trial separation is simply a precursor to divorce. But in some cases a temporary split can give you both the opportunity to take a step back, regain some perspective, and see how you really feel. It's suffocating to live in an environment that's become fraught with tension, and time apart can let you breathe.

Here's an idea for you . . .

If separation is on the cards for you, set an initial time period of two to six months, after which you will review how it's going. You need to agree on a time that suits you both, as well as what the rules of your separation will be. That way you'll both be happy that you're entering into the separation seriously and with mutual consent. Write your agreement down and stick to it. Set a date when the separation starts and when you'll review things again.

We all know that it's difficult to make rational decisions in the heat of an argument and making the decision as to whether to divorce or not needs careful thought and calm consideration. Trial separation can take the heat out of the conflict and removes the opportunity for day-to-day bickering and accusations.

Make sure you are clear about your intentions with your partner. If you're simply using the separation as a gentle way into divorce, then it's better to start divorce proceedings right away. That way you remove any false hope and extra hurt from the situation.

DECISION TIME

Deciding if a temporary split is right for you can be agonizing. So how can you make sure you're doing the right thing? Well, have a look at the questions below, and if your answer to four or more of them is "yes," then a trial separation is worth considering.

- Do you always fight when you try to talk about your problems?
- Do you constantly argue about trivial things?
- Do you feel like you're going around in circles and there's no way out?
- Is your relationship making you ill or depressed?
- Are your children suffering from the problems in your marriage?
- Is there abuse, gambling, or addiction involved?
- Do you fantasize about being alone?

If you have answered yes to four or more of the questions: What next? As with everything, preparation is key. Start by explaining what you want in a calm, straightforward way and give your spouse time to absorb your suggestion. A trial separation will only work if you both agree to it.

Does a trial separation feel a bit drastic? Then look at IDEA 21, *Stop hating, start communicating*, and see if counseling could be the option for you.

Try another idea . . .

Plan what you are going to do about living arrangements and finances. If you have children, who will they stay with and how much access will they have to the other parent? Decide whether you will see each other during the separation. Will you be free to date other people, or will you remain monogamous? How long will you separate for, and when will you review the situation? If all these questions are addressed calmly and sensibly, and amicable agreements are made, then your trial split has every chance of working well.

A trial separation may be the last chance for your marriage, but it could also hold the solution to your problems. Never assume a positive or negative outcome, and so put pressure on the split. At the very least, some time alone will give you both an opportunity to work out whether you prefer being together or apart.

If you do decide to get back together, make sure you base this on a firm foundation and not simply a rekindled spark of romance. Ask yourself what has changed? What is different?

"If you love somebody let them go. If they return they were always yours. If they don't they never were."
CONFUCIUS

Defining idea . . .

How can you maintain that change? Slipping back into your old way of life will restore old routines and old habits, and that will lead to old problems. Constantly review and maintain your marriage and be aware that it has been to the brink and back.

How did it go?

Q   My wife has asked for a trial separation and I've agreed. But how am I going to cope? We've always done everything together.

A   *Maybe doing too much together has been one of your problems. Use this time to get to know yourself as an individual again. What would you like to do? Enjoy this space and allow yourself to grow, not pine away. That way, if you get back together you'll have something new to bring to the relationship. And if you stay apart, you'll have laid the foundations for a new life.*

Q   My husband and I separated for six months and decided to get back together. How can I make it feel different this time?

A   *Ensure you don't fall back into old habits. Take up a hobby together instead of watching TV on Monday night. Take a weekend break every six weeks. Treat your marriage carefully and tend to it regularly. Why not take a second honeymoon or renew your wedding vows? A special event is a good way to cement your renewed commitment to each other.*

13

Cutting ties

Cutting the ties with your ex needn't mean scissors snapping through silk. But if the knots between you would confuse a naval cadet, then you need to start unraveling them to move on.

Ties that bind can be cut even if they can't be unraveled. Rather than dwelling on the past and trying to unknot the history between you, focus on the future. Your divorce is the sharpest tool in your box. It can cut through even the most restrictive bondage of marriage.

GET KNOTTED!

It's a fact that marriage ties you together as a couple. It binds you close and interweaves almost every aspect of your life. However, when things start to go wrong, the small threads between you start to snap. As you pull further apart, even the stronger ties are stretched to the limit, and divorce breaks them for good. Or does it? It can be surprisingly difficult to sever connections with a former spouse, especially if the divorce wasn't a mutual choice.

Here's an idea for you . . .

Weekends and evenings can be lonely for the recently divorced and you may find your fingers itching with the desire to call your ex. But don't scratch! The more contact you have, the harder it will be to move on. Concentrate on your friendships. Plan your weekends well in advance and anticipate your lonely times. Devise a list of activities that can instantly be brought into play. Remember, if you're socializing with friends who have remained mutual, avoid asking for information about your ex. This will place them in a difficult position or they may tell you things you don't want to hear.

Of course, if you have children there will always be a connection between you both. But that connection shouldn't be a tie that holds you back from your new future. If you do have a friendship with your ex this can make things a lot easier for coparenting, but make sure your feelings remain platonic. It's easy to fall back into the comfortable intimacy of marriage, but this can be very destructive to one party if the other doesn't feel the same way.

LOOSE ENDS

The ties between a married couple are both practical and emotional. Some are easy to cut and others are far more resistant to the scissors of divorce. Often the best way to cut the emotional bonds between you and your ex is to ensure that all the practical arrangements between you are tied up securely.

Money matters can tie you up in knots for years if not dealt with quickly and efficiently. To avoid this, a good attorney should be consulted to ensure you get the fairest deal. Once you have reached a settlement, stick to it and tie up the loose ends as quickly as possible. Arrange for all joint accounts to be closed and make certain that you have current, individual accounts in place. Check through all direct debits, standing orders, and credit cards to be sure the correct person is paying them, and cancel any that are redundant.

If you think cutting ties really is just about fraying fabric with a pair of pinking shears, then take a look at IDEA 18, *The backlash*, for some less drastic approaches.

Try another idea . . .

Your house will be seen as part of your marital assets and considered in any financial settlement. However, even if the marital home has been awarded to you, ask yourself if you really want to stay there. If you are having problems moving on from your marriage, remaining in the home you shared with your ex could be a bad decision. The home will be full of memories, good and bad, so consider a move to cut through the strong emotional echoes of living alone in your marital home.

Custody of your children, visitation, and their maintenance will be a key part of your divorce. If your children are having any contact with your ex, then there will be an unavoidable tie that remains between you. However, try to see this as positive. Divorced parents can still be good parents and in this case some degree of partnership may be a good thing. However, if you find it painful or just downright irritating to be connected to your ex, focus on your children. Ensure that all contact and conversation you have is about your children. Avoid involvement in other aspects of each other's lives as this will make moving on far harder.

"The turning point in the process of growing up is when you discover the core of strength within you that survives all hurt."
MAX WERNER, writer

Defining idea . . .

51

How did it go?

Q How can I cut the ties with my ex-husband when we've been together since we were teenagers?

A *First accept that it will be hard and it will take time. Then deal with practicalities. Reinstate your maiden name; this will give you a greater sense of your individual identity. Focus on all the things that make you unique and separate—your job, your clothes, your interests. Develop and experiment with these and you'll soon find the individual who got tied down in the marriage.*

Q It's my son's graduation and his mother and I are going through an acrimonious divorce. How can I be supportive for him when I'm sure I'll end up shouting at her?

A *It's your son's special day, and nothing should get in the way of that. But don't expect to play happy families. That tie has been cut. Talk to your son and find a way to be there without triggering World War Three. Perhaps you could sit separately at the graduation. If your son is desperate for a family photo, grit your teeth and smile. But refuse to be drawn into conversations regarding the divorce, and avoid a family meal. Instead, arrange to take your son out individually, before or after the event.*

14

Dating dilemmas

Met someone you just can't resist? Or maybe you'd just like to get out there and have some fun for a change. Whatever your situation, you need to know the pros and cons of dating during divorce.

Just about everything you read regarding dating during divorce is negative. In fact I'm surprised that great whooping alarms don't sound whenever you combine "dating + divorce" in an Internet search! However, is that the final word?

IS IT ROMANCE OR RATTLESNAKE FOOTBALL?

Theoretically, there is no reason why a date before the divorce is final should be as risky as playing barefoot football with a rattlesnake. Let's face it, hundreds of people will date during the divorce process, so we may as well acknowledge that and ensure it's done as positively as possible.

Here's an idea for you . . .

Going on a date? Then make sure you're not a divorce bore. It's a trap that many people fall into and end up wondering why their dates didn't want to see them again. So instead of droning on your date about the sins of your evil ex-to-be, remember that you're supposed to be having fun. This will be much easier to do if you choose an activity for your date that can also be the focus of your conversation—a film, a trip to the theater, or a sporting event will provide a mutual experience that you can chat about over drinks later.

First of all, it's important to recognize the difference between "dating" and "cohabiting." If you cohabit with another person before the divorce is final, you could be asking for a legal headache. Cohabitation may sound like something a tortoise does in November in a cardboard box stuffed with newspaper, but it is just the legal term for living together. In other words, you're sharing your place of residence and expenses with another person. There doesn't even have to be any salacious stuff going on for it to negatively affect your case. The court may feel that because you are sharing your expenses with another, you will have more funds available to contribute in maintenance.

And vice versa. If you are the spouse to receive maintenance and you are sharing that cosy cardboard box with another tortoise, your need for maintenance may be viewed as less, and payments to you may be reduced accordingly.

Cohabitation prior to divorce can also affect child maintenance payments and visitation. A court will always place your child's emotional well-being before your own. Therefore, if it considers your cohabitation with a new partner to be detrimental to the child's emotions, it will rule accordingly.

The second thing to consider is your spouse's reaction. If there is any kind of bad feeling between you—and let's face it, divorces are rarely full of chummy smiles—they may see your new relationship as ammunition, both in court and out of it.

So you'd like to date but you feel you look more like your mailman George than George Clooney? Look at IDEA 25, *Body beautiful*, to banish those negative thoughts.

Try another idea . . .

Be aware that the more manipulative of partners will take any opportunity to vent their anger and take their revenge. So keep your personal life to yourself. If you don't, you may need to keep your personal items well clear of sharp scissors.

FOLLOW THE RULES

If you follow a few simple rules, it's easy to make dating during divorce both safe and fun.

- **Rule 1 is to assess the amount of risk involved and act accordingly**. So if your ex-to-be is more savage over the divorce than a starving hyena on a fat wildebeest, then be careful. If you've already gotten the petition accepted on the grounds you have requested, it may be easier for you to date safely.

- **Rule 2 is to question your motives.** Why do you want to date? Perhaps you've been separated for a long time and it's time to move on. Maybe you just need some laughs and want a bit of flattery from the opposite sex after years of being in a marriage that makes *The Sopranos* look like a comedy. If that's the case then great,

"I usually avoid temptation, unless I can't resist it."
MAE WEST

Defining idea . . .

go ahead and date. But if you want to date solely to make your ex-to-be jealous then it's time for a rethink!

- **Rule 3 is to keep things simple.** Date for fun, not to find the next partner of your dreams. So if someone's asked you out for a drink, then go out for just that; banish any thoughts that this date could be "the one."

Dating during divorce is a tricky issue but, if you follow the guidelines, a little companionship with the opposite sex might be just what you need to lift your spirits. Just keep it light. Dating during an already emotionally stressful time in your life should be treated with caution and respect, but not with fear. If you are frightened that your dates might jeopardize your divorce, then don't date, wait!

How did it go?

Q **My divorce is lasting so long that I'll have my retirement party before my next date. Is it legal to date before divorce?**

A   *If you haven't got your official decree of divorce you are still legally married. Therefore, if you have sexual relations with someone other than your spouse it can be seen as adultery.*

Q **Do I tell my date I'm in the middle of a divorce?**

A   *Yes. It's always best to be honest. Be frank but keep things as light as you can. If your date feels uncomfortable with the situation, then you can simply agree not to see each other again.*

15

Mediation, not litigation

Here's the situation: neither of you will budge, you've said all there is to say, and you still can't agree on a settlement. You're going straight to court, right? Wrong! There's another possibility—mediation, and it could help you.

Even if you feel like you're banging your head against a brick wall, mediation can be the key to finding that elusive compromise. It's far less expensive than litigation—and certainly a lot less painful than the head-banging approach.

TAKING THE STING OUT OF YOUR DIVORCE

Poised halfway along the motorway that runs from counseling to court, mediation is a service station that's being visited frequently as divorces become increasingly complex. Mediation doesn't pretend to be a form of therapy or a path to reconciliation; it is firmly aimed at couples whose relationship has already broken down irretrievably. It's a bit like a trade union arbitration service for battling spouses: both parties are given the time and opportunity to voice their views and opinions while a third party chairs the discussion.

Here's an idea for you . . .

Make a list of the topics that are frustrating the hell out of you and your ex-to-be, then give them to a mediator and start to take back control. Examples might include:

- **Custody and visitation rights regarding children**
- **Ongoing parenting responsibilities—in other words, how decisions regarding education and upbringing will be reached in the future**
- **Housing requirements for both parties**
- **Division of marital possessions, including the home**
- **Financial support and settlement**

Use mediation to remove the venom from the snakebite of divorce.

Why might you need mediation? You've agreed to divorce and there's no way you're going to get back together, so why not go straight to an attorney and get it over with? That sounds fair enough—in fact, an attorney will be required to legalize any agreement you reach during mediation. However, if you can't agree with your spouse about anything at all, and every time you talk to each other you end up hoarse from shouting, then your legal fees are set to be astronomical. So, if that is the case, mediation could save you a lot of time and money (not to mention saving your larynx, too).

Quite often in the process of divorce we feel that our spouse refuses to listen to our views and dismisses our needs. Reasonable discussions escalate rapidly to thermonuclear arguments, and most of the possessions we're arguing over are flung against walls in frustration. Mediation can prevent this from happening, and can also stop your private battles from becoming public news at the local court.

MEDIATION'S ON THE MENU

Over the past twenty years, mediation has become the latest addition to the menu of divorce services available and it covers a wide range of circumstances. If you'd like to solve your issues yourselves, rather than getting the court to do it for you, then mediation is definitely a good option.

So, you'd like to try to sort things out without a mediator, but the question of who gets the family home is proving tricky. Look at IDEA 36, *Your place or mine?*, for some useful advice.

Try another idea . . .

Even couples who part amicably can hit stumbling blocks when it comes to discussing emotive issues regarding arrangements for children and money. It's easy to find yourselves going around in circles trying and failing to agree on arrangements for the divorce. But let's face it: if you got along so well that discussions on subjects covering the essential elements of life were that easy, then you probably wouldn't be getting divorced anyway.

The mediation process allows you as a couple to set the agenda for either one or a number of discussions, and one or sometimes two trained mediators will act as a chairperson and referee. The mediators can't give you legal advice, but they can ensure you get the opportunity to focus on the issues that are important to you. They can help you avoid unnecessary legal confrontation and will also allow you to be heard and acknowledged.

"The best way out is always through."
ROBERT FROST

Defining idea . . .

The training of mediators is now regulated in many countries and is a well-regarded service often run in conjunction with court proceedings. Mediation is a great way of taking control of a potentially acrimonious situation. It gives the divorcing couple the power to reach their own agreements and not have to settle for those imposed on them by a judge in court. The couple can leave the marriage feeling that, although it didn't work out, communication was possible and an amicable solution was reached.

How did it go?

Q How can a mediator help us when even I can't work out what I want and need from my divorce settlement?

A   *Even if your finances are more complicated than Fermat's last theorem, a mediator is trained to go through your assets with you to help reach the best decision for both spouses. In your case, perhaps a trip to an accountant to see exactly what your assets amount to may be a good bet. That way you can take some facts and figures with you to the mediation meeting.*

Q I hate my wife; we don't agree on anything. How can a mediator help with that?

A   *A mediator can't help you with the problems that led to your divorce: they aren't trained to be counselors. What a mediator can do, however, is help you agree on the practical issues regarding your separation without letting the anger and bad feelings get in the way.*

16

Covering grounds

Maybe your reasons for wanting a divorce are as simple as ABC. Or maybe they're so complex you'd need the whole alphabet to describe them? Whatever your situation, your reasons must tie in with the legal grounds for a petition.

Adultery? Abuse? Irreconcilable differences? Have a look below for a pick-and-mix guide to covering grounds.

A WALK IN THE PARK, OR AN UPHILL STRUGGLE?

The dissolution of a marriage is rarely a smooth ride and will usually cover some very rough terrain. Let's face it, no one goes through the process of divorce for fun and most of us get shaken up along the way. But there are lots of ways in which you can begin to smooth out the path in front of you. As with anything in life, knowing your facts and preparing yourself in advance is essential if you want to avoid any nasty surprises later on.

So, are you prepared? You probably think you are—after all, the reasons you're getting a divorce are simple: he's a slob, she's a nag, and you can't stand the sight of each other anymore. Any judge in the country would understand why you don't

Here's an idea for you . . .

Be your own investigator. In order to make the process of divorce as straightforward as possible, gather all the evidence you can for your petition. If you're divorcing on grounds of adultery, make sure that your spouse will admit to it, or, if not, gather any evidence you think you might need in court. Bank statements, credit card bills, or vacation booking confirmations can all help. For grounds of abuse, list dates, times, and episodes and get supporting statements if necessary.

want to lie next to your snoring wife or your smelly husband a moment longer, wouldn't they? Well, if you put it like that, no!

Sometimes the reasons why we want to divorce our spouse seem perfectly logical to us, but they may not fit into the legal parameters that are known as "grounds." Of course, many of us are unlucky enough to have very clear reasons, such as our spouse's infidelity. In this case, the grounds for petition become obvious. But for others the grounds for divorce are more misty. For example, "jealousy" and "nagging" don't appear as legal grounds, but they are seen as valid reasons that can lead to the erosion and ultimate breakdown of a marriage.

Let's look at exactly how you can turn your reasons to separate into "grounds for divorce."

DOING THE GROUNDWORK

It's relatively easy to do the groundwork for your divorce by researching exactly what grounds are relevant to the divorce laws where you live. The Internet is a great way to do this, but here are a few examples that may help you to get started.

Adultery is among the most popular reasons for divorce. If your spouse is having consensual sex (with his consent, not yours) with anyone other than you, you have every right to file for divorce on grounds of adultery. Infidelity can be particularly hard to prove if your spouse contests it, though, so any evidence you can produce will be essential to your petition.

Desertion, while rare, is also grounds for divorce. And like adultery, desertion can be tricky to prove. The spouse's leaving must be intentional and permanent, and he must also manage to keep his whereabouts secret from the family. You must be able to prove that your spouse has purposely disappeared, and that you have made unsuccessful efforts to locate him.

Abuse is another common ground for divorce. Petitioning under these grounds may require that you state specific incidences of when your spouse's behavior has been so bad that you can no longer live with him. Examples include physical, emotional, or psychological violence. Your spouse must acknowledge these as true, otherwise it will need to be proven in court.

> If you and your spouse have agreed on the grounds for divorce between you and are planning an amicable split, have a look at IDEA 6, *DIY divorce*, and do it the inexpensive way.

Try another idea . . .

> *"If it isn't a success, that still wouldn't be grounds for divorce."*
> GEENA DAVIS

Defining idea . . .

63

The purpose of citing a ground for divorce on your petition papers is to prove to the court that your marriage has broken down irretrievably. In other words, you've tried to save your relationship but the problems within it can't be solved.

Being clear and precise when stating your grounds for petition can save a lot of hassle later in the divorce proceedings.

How did it go?

Q   Can my spouse prevent the court from granting us a divorce?

A   *Your spouse cannot oppose a no-fault divorce, as the disagreement would constitute an indication of fault. Your spouse can prevent a fault divorce, however, by proving that he is not guilty of whatever fault you present as grounds. He can counter your grounds with a defense of collusion (you conspired with him to deceive the court), condonation (saying you condoned the activities in question), connivance (you set him up to commit the fault), or provocation (you provoked him to do it).*

Q   Can I petition for divorce if my husband and I haven't slept with each other for six years?

A   *A complaint like this might fall under the category of "irreconcilable differences," which is an acceptable ground for no-fault divorce.*

17

Healing hands

Divorce saps our energy. It makes us tired, cynical, and miserable. Even the strongest and most positive among us can be hurt and exhausted by the end of divorce proceedings. We need a tonic.

Feeling down? Depressed? Distressed? Well, don't, because there is no reason why these feelings have to last. Take a look below to see how a little alternative thought can help you to heal.

Divorce often ends up all about money: maintenance from you or for you, payments for the kids, the attorneys' fees, the court costs, the Realtor's fees—the list goes on. But what about the emotional cost? It may well empty your marital coffers, but you don't want it to leave you feeling empty inside, too.

Now maybe the only healing hands you want on you are those of your new girl- or boyfriend. But not all of us are that lucky. Perhaps you're a bit wary of all that alternative "healing" stuff and would rather just go clubbing. But if you're all

Here's an idea for you . . .

Cleanse your chakras. Chakras are central to all energy healing and have been referred to in mysticism and oriental and Asiatic medicine for centuries. Simply put, they are the centers of energy that run along the midline of the body. There are seven chakras that relate to psychological and physical properties, and two of them, the heart chakra and the throat chakra, frequently become affected during divorce. The heart because of your emotional pain, and the throat because you may have trouble expressing yourself. Many therapists can cleanse your chakras using massage and reiki, but you can start your own cleansing routine at home. Begin by practicing deep breathing in a relaxed setting for two sessions of five minutes each day to oxygenate your body and free your mind. Massage your stomach in a circular motion to stimulate digestion. This will get you started on a holistic approach to healing.

clubbed out and talked out but you're still stressed out, why not have a look at something different?

For example, diamonds don't have to remind you of engagement rings. "Crystal healing" is a form of energy healing that realigns the imbalances of energy in your body that can lead to emotional and physical *dis-ease*. Crystals are used to channel positive energy into your body to cleanse and heal your chakras.

"Reiki," pronounced *ray-kee*, is another form of alternative healing and not something you do in the yard with a pile of leaves in October! It's a form of energy healing that can help heal both physical and emotional problems. Here, it's the therapist's hands that channel the healing energy. This energy is referred to as *chi*, a Chinese word that refers to the energy that underpins all things physical and emotional in the world. Reiki is used to strengthen your *aura* by purifying and positively guiding the energy that is naturally present in your body.

If you're more into *Star Wars* than mystic thought, consider all this energy stuff as The Force. It's easier! Okay, maybe you'd rather reinforce your energy with a bottle of Gatorade, but what if your divorce has stolen all your laughter, and even the Three Stooges can't make you crack a smile? Then it's time to get your grin back.

Okay, so you're still not convinced. Take a look at IDEA 42, *Spas, bars, and chocolate*, for a more traditional approach to beating the blues.

Try another idea . . .

GET YOUR GIGGLE BACK!

If divorce has wiped the smile off your face, then why not try some *laughter yoga*? (See, you're giggling already—I told you it would work!) Laughter yoga, also known as *Hasya yoga*, was developed in 1995 by Dr. Madan Kataria, a physician from Mumbai, India. There are now over 2,000 laughter clubs worldwide and the practice has been documented in mainstream publications such as the *Times*, *Wall Street Journal*, and *National Geographic* magazine.

Dr. Kataria was trained in conventional yoga as well as medicine, but felt that both were lacking when it came to healing the emotions. He felt that there was a great need to remove negative emotions such as anger, fear, jealousy, and sadness—the emotions that can lead to stress-related illnesses.

Now we all know that laughing releases tension. But what happens if the circumstances, such as your divorce, mean that laughing comes as naturally to you as space travel? Dr. Kataria recognized this problem and used the breathing principles of traditional yoga to get his clients giggling again.

"By taking this action, I hope I will have hastened the start of healing."
RICHARD NIXON

Defining idea . . .

67

You need no jokes, no comedy, and nothing in particular to laugh about. Quite simply, the breathing exercises are guided into simulated laughter. It starts with "ho-ho, hum-hum" techniques before the group practices "lion laughter [which I presume is a bit of a roar!], hearty laughter, and silent laughter," as well as quite a few you've never even heard of. Very soon the laughter stops being simulated and becomes natural. Each member of the group is encouraged to practice laughter for 15–20 minutes a day. Laughter yoga has achieved astounding results in lifting depression in India and worldwide.

How did it go?

Q   How can I try something like energy healing when I thought my chakra was my local Indian restaurant?

A   *Many spas offer elements of reiki as part of their massage treatments. Try that first in familiar, conventional surroundings and see how you get on.*

Q   How easy is it to find a laughter yoga course?

A   *Laughter yoga is growing in popularity. Have a look online and talk to your local yoga teacher—often found in sports centers and adult education centers. If that doesn't turn up anything for you, get hold of a book on the subject and practice the laughter techniques yourself or with friends.*

18

The backlash

The grief's gone and now you just want to shred his suits and mangle her Manolos. The backlash from divorce can have a nasty sting. Stop your passion from turning into poison.

Revenge is sweet! Or so you might think. Actually, the understandable bitterness that's driving your desire for revenge is a very negative emotion that could destroy you. Control the anger or you'll never move on.

HOT PASSION, COLD REVENGE

Most of us will remember the story of John Wayne Bobbitt who shot to fame in 1993 after his wife, Loretta, cut off his penis and threw it from her car window. Mrs. Bobbitt's actions were later considered by a court to be the result of insanity and she avoided a prison sentence.

Less dramatic acts of revenge occur in marriages all over the world. Through various friends and acquaintances I've heard a remarkably varied list of ways to take revenge on an ex-partner. Itching powder in underpants, false emails inviting hundreds of

Here's an idea for you . . .

Write a pledge to yourself that you won't demonize your ex. If you break the pledge, it will only fuel your anger. A friend of mine constantly drew cartoons of his ex as a monster with Dracula-like fangs sucking at his bank account. Although this was quite funny for his friends, it made him feel a lot worse. After a while he realized he could use his talents to help him get rid of his anger. So he started to draw cartoons of his ex as a useless, spineless jellyfish way below him in the food chain who couldn't harm a fly. After a few weeks of doing this he found that his anger had faded and he felt far better. His ex was less threatening and he felt better equipped to move on with his life without being crippled by anger toward his former wife.

people to the ex's house for a party they know nothing about, or shredding your ex's clothes are just a few choice selections!

Although we may start to snigger at some of these pranks, some acts of revenge can become serious and threatening. The partner contemplating revenge may actually be seriously depressed by the breakup and unable to come to terms with the reality of being alone.

The desire for revenge is a perfectly natural reaction, especially if your partner cheated on you, or you didn't want to get divorced in the first place. But it's interesting to note that the feelings of anger you get when you start to yearn for revenge have much the same physical effect on your body as being passionately in love—your heart rate increases, you start to sweat, your blood pressure goes up, and adrenaline pumps through your body. You must try to control yourself before your anger controls you.

CONTROL YOURSELF!

Being angry with your ex is a normal part of getting through the breakup—you may feel betrayed, hurt, and frustrated—but it's important not to let these angry feelings grow and get in the way of your new life. If you are seriously considering revenge, then it's time for a bit of anger management.

Maybe you just need a laugh. Laughing is excellent for releasing tension, so have a look at IDEA 17, *Healing hands*, and give laughter yoga a try.

Try another idea . . .

Anger management is a practical way of managing your anger and frustration before it becomes a problem and can be used during, as well as after, the divorce. The first stage of managing your anger about a situation is acknowledging that it exists. Of course you can still be angry about what's happened to you—anger management is not about pretending that everything in your life is like a Disney film. However, instead of ranting and raving, you need to learn positive ways of expressing the anger and achieving your goals. The key here is to be *assertive* not *aggressive*. As soon as you feel your anger starting to kick in and your fingers itching to take the pinking shears to clothes, your anger management strategies should kick in.

Most important is to try to stay calm. This can be done in a number of ways. For example, deep breathing exercises will help to lower your heart rate and blood pressure. Then repeat a calming phrase such as "She's not worth the anger, I'm in control." Try visualizing a calming image, such as a tropical sea or a gentle breeze moving through a field of corn. If this doesn't work, think of a humorous situation or joke that always makes you smile.

"If you are patient in a moment of anger you will escape 1,000 years of sorrow."
CHINESE PROVERB

Defining idea . . .

71

Anger shouldn't be repressed, but it should be vented in a controlled way. Suppressing your feelings can often be negative, especially if you redirect your anger at your ex toward yourself. Learn to express yourself in a logical and calm way. If you need to scream and shout then do so, but not at your partner. Find a quiet room and yell as much as you like. And, please, put away those scissors!

How did it go?

Q   All these relaxation techniques don't work for me. How can I stop my anger from making me feel like a coiled spring?

A   Exercise. Relaxation techniques are useful, but you need a way to get rid of all that frustrated energy. Try a run or a game of football. The endorphins exercise releases will make you feel happy, not homicidal.

Q   What else can I do? I've tried it all—relaxation, exercise, reasoning—and I still want to shred every suit he owns!

A   Try writing your feelings down. You can either vent your frustrations in a diary, or write a short story where the "fictional you" does all the things you'd like to but can't. Making it fiction, not fact, will be cathartic but safe.

19

Are you speaking my language?

The difference between men and women when it comes to the issue of communication is relevant to all stages of a relationship. Amid the deafening conflict of a divorce, communicating in words you can both understand is even more essential.

We've all heard that men are from Mars and women are from Venus, but at least those two planets are in the same solar system. Anyone who's going through a divorce knows that men and women are probably from completely different galaxies!

BUILD YOUR OWN SPACESHIP

Sometimes talking to aliens might seem an easier option than talking to your spouse. A friend of mine always said that English was her husband's second

Here's an idea for you . . .

It's important to realize that men and women communicate in different ways. So, men, when you're next having a discussion with your wife, actively reassure her that you are listening to her and thinking about what she says. Maintain eye contact and don't move around the room when she's talking. Try to wait until she's finished speaking before giving her your views and make specific references to what she's said. Women, *accept* that your man reacts to relationship issues in a different way and may not need to talk about stuff as much as you. So if he needs space to think things through before a discussion, then simply give him that time. Tell him you are available to talk, but don't force him to as he'll feel resentful. Instead explain calmly that if he can vocalize his needs, it will be a lot easier for you to meet them.

language after farting and snoring. Her husband in turn was convinced that if he could master communicating only through crying and throwing things, they'd be a very happy couple.

The fact is that women and men naturally communicate in different ways. Their needs for communication are different and they use different ways of expressing themselves. The thing to remember is that you are both speaking the *same language*, but you're just using *different words*. You need to understand each other's "relationship vocabulary" rather than expect your partner to use yours. Sounds about as easy as learning Ancient Greek by next Friday, doesn't it? Well, it's far easier, I promise. It's just a matter of perception.

VIVE LA DIFFERENCE

Women, you think you've been doing all the work, don't you? After all, you've been expressing yourself openly, describing your feelings, taking every opportunity to talk things through. But even after all that, you haven't got much back, have you? Well the reason for that might be that you haven't left him much room to say anything. Any "relationship discussion" has an allotted amount of time that will naturally run out depending on both of your levels of tolerance and concentration. Generally, women last longer. But, by the time they've finished their bit, how much time is left for the man?

Are you finding everything tough to talk about, including your sex life? Take a look at IDEA 2, *Maybe the va-va-voom can work for you*, for some tips and tricks.

Try another idea . . .

Instead of giving a long speech, which will bore your man rigid, try to be precise and focus on the main points. If it helps, make a list of what you want to discuss and stick to it. Be clear about what you're saying, why you're saying it, and what you want out of the discussion. And remember it's a discussion, not a lecture.

Men, you need to realize that women *need* to talk about things, especially their feelings. Women aren't always looking for an answer to their problems. I know you think you're helping when you offer a practical solution after the first three minutes of her talking, and then, after you've been helpful, she starts to cry and says you don't understand her. Baffling! Well, not really. Your woman wants to talk things through, to communicate how she feels and have you acknowledge her emotions. She doesn't always want you to solve things.

Men and women have been caught up in a war of communication since the first caveman looked at the first cavewoman and said "phwoar!" She rolled her eyes to the sky, adjusted her loincloth, and went out to walk the mammoth. Caveman did a double take and wondered what he'd said wrong.

"When two people decide to divorce it isn't a sign they don't understand each other, but a sign that they have at last begun to!"
HELEN ROWLAND, journalist

Defining idea . . .

Unfortunately, divorce can often be a final battleground for that timeless war of words. But even if your relationship has broken down, acknowledging that men and women communicate differently will definitely lower the casualty rate during the war.

How did it go?

Q   **How can I make my husband tell me the truth about his feelings? Whenever he's quiet and I ask him what he's thinking about, he says "football"!**

A   *Have you considered the fact that he is telling you the truth? You may want him to be thinking about the finer points of your marriage, but he's probably thinking about the offside rule. Accept that men think differently from women, and if you want him to think about an issue in your relationship, be specific. Ask him to think about that issue and arrange to discuss it at a mutually acceptable time.*

Q   **How can I stop my wife from trying to change the way I communicate? I do want it to work, but all this touchy-feely stuff isn't for me.**

A   *Perhaps there is a middle ground. Explain to your wife that you feel uncomfortable using emotional language—and don't say "touchy-feely," as this might provoke an argument. Tell her you are committed to making the relationship work, but you need to be able to express yourself in language you feel comfortable with. Once you have acknowledged and accepted her need to talk, the words used will be less important.*

20

Baggage handling

Is the baggage from your marriage portable? Or does moving it take an army of porters? Whether it's the emotional equivalent of a Louis Vuitton trunk or a battered old briefcase you've been carrying around for ages, everyone has baggage to handle after a divorce.

The aim of this idea is to help you stow your baggage in the hold so you can continue your journey without being crushed under the weight of it at the emotional luggage carousel.

BAGGAGE CHECK

The first thing to realize is that all people have baggage, whether they've been through a divorce or not. Think of all the places you've visited in your lifetime and all the souvenirs and photos you picked up along the way—well, it's exactly the same with our emotions.

Every relationship we have leaves us with some kind of emotional impact. The most important element of ensuring that baggage is manageable is to do a baggage

Here's an idea for you . . .

The idea here is to show your scars. Be honest about the negative baggage that you haul around with you. Flag areas that concern you the most. For example, if your wife left you for another man, tell your partner you know that you'll need to watch your jealousy and ask her for her understanding. This approach could keep minor issues from escalating into major arguments.

check. This won't involve a metal detector and a sniffer dog, but it will require a few security questions. After your divorce do you feel that:

- You can't trust anyone again?
- No one cares about you and never will?
- Everyone else is selfish?
- You're the victim?

If you do, then you're certainly carrying over your baggage allowance, and you'll have to leave some of it behind. It may well be true that you've been hurt or treated badly during your marriage, but just because this has happened once doesn't mean it has to happen again.

There are many steps you can take to prevent previous baggage from weighing down a new relationship. Make sure that you're not superimposing the faults of your ex onto your new partner. Sure, they may have more faults than a school spelling test, but they might not be the *same* ones as your former spouse. If you truly have found a carbon copy of your ex, then the sooner you realize your mistake and move on, the better.

It's also important to take responsibility for your own part in the breakdown of your marriage. We all mess up in love and it's more common that a relationship has failed because of *both* of you rather than just one. Acknowledging the part you played will help you avoid making the same mistakes in the future.

TRASH IT!

But maybe you blame yourself too much. Perhaps you're spending so much time beating yourself up that there's no room left in your life for a new relationship. If that's true for you, then it's time to trash your baggage and stop carrying it around with you.

If you're managing your emotional baggage now, but you've still got concerns about tying the knot again, have a look at IDEA 34, *Second time around*, and jilt your jitters.

Try another idea . . .

We've all heard that it's important to forgive and forget, and that goes for forgiving yourself, too. Even if it was your fault, the marriage is over and you must accept that and move on. All baggage is essentially life experience, and you need to learn from it and then let it go.

Not all the experiences we had in our marriage were bad. In your case, is the baggage you have so heavy because you can't get over your ex? Was he or she so great in your mind that there's no way your new partner will be able to meet your expectations? The harsh fact you must face is that even if your ex was pretty fantastic, he or she is still just that—your *ex*! So if there's no hope of a reconciliation, it's time to move on. For whatever reasons, the marriage failed, and that means you and your partner were not the perfect match despite your expectations.

However heavy your baggage is, and however good or bad it looks, it's time to empty the suitcase of your marriage. That way there'll be plenty of room to store the experiences you and your new partner will have together.

"Everyone has baggage. It's how you carry it that counts."
MODERN PROVERB

Defining idea . . .

How did it go?

Q **I'm divorced. How wise is it to start a serious relationship with someone who's recently gone through a divorce herself?**

A *You're probably thinking that two sets of divorce baggage will weigh doubly heavy on you both emotionally. This isn't necessarily true. Baggage is essentially experience, and divorce is an experience you both have in common. You may well have a deeper understanding of each other simply because you've gone through the same process. Feelings of hurt, anger, betrayal, and sadness will be familiar to both of you, and this common experience may create a deeper bond.*

Q **How much time should I give to discussing my old relationship baggage with my new partner?**

A *Keep it to a minimum but, as I've said, you should show your scars and make your new partner aware of your issues. Don't dwell on them, though. Using the baggage of your past as an excuse for negative patterns of behavior today will spell the end of a new relationship. Own your baggage, but don't let it own you.*

21

Stop hating, start communicating

Your idea of a counselor might be Hannibal Lecter in a cardigan, but if your partner's become more Martian than mate and you're hating the communication breakdown, then it might be the time to give a counseling service a try.

Good communication really is the key to a successful marriage and, conversely, a successful divorce. Before, during, or after divorce, talking things through with a third party can be invaluable.

RELATING TO EACH OTHER

At all stages in a relationship, being able to communicate your needs and feelings to a partner who will listen to you is vital. I know what you're thinking—you've tried to communicate in so many ways and your partner still won't change. You can't understand why he won't even try to sort out the problems that plague your relationship, and you don't see the point in trying anymore.

Here's an idea for you . . . **Can't face seeing a counselor? Then do it on the phone. Many counseling services offer telephone consultations. The telephone service allows you to access counseling even if you are in a different location from your partner by means of a conference call. It also solves the problem of needing to find childcare if you're both out of the house, and it also offers after-hours consultations. Online consultations are also available.**

If communication is defunct, then it becomes impossible to understand each other's points of view. As soon as you reach this point, you lose the ability to compromise or accommodate your spouse's needs, and that's when the relationship really starts to crumble.

Maybe you can't fix the problems yourself but perhaps someone else can. If your car breaks down you may open up the hood, tinker, and tweak a few things, but if that doesn't work you call in someone to help. It's highly unlikely that you would abandon your car by the roadside, walk off, and forget it just because you aren't trained to fix it yourself.

It's exactly the same with a relationship. Maybe you've tried to fix it and you haven't succeeded. In that case, now's the time to call in the professionals; people who are trained to help you put your relationship back together—relationship counselors.

THE GOOD GUYS!

Over the years, counselors have been saddled with a rather bad image. Many of us think they'll be off-puttingly dressed—probably favoring the sort of sweater your great auntie gives you at Christmas every year—and have a penchant for facial hair and clipboards. Just remember that counselors come from all walks of life, they are of all ages, and they are trained to deal with every kind of relationship issue imaginable.

You can't shock a counselor. They, like doctors, have heard it all before. If your relationship problems are sexual, there is no need to be embarrassed. Sex is central to a marriage, and all problems related to it are handled with sensitivity and care. Your sessions with a counselor are also strictly confidential. Counselors realize that you will not share intimate details, arguments, and your hopes and fears with someone who might blab about them later at the bar.

If you've decided to divorce, look at IDEA 15, *Mediation, not litigation*, and counsel yourself through the next stage.

Try another idea . . .

Now that you understand that they're the good guys, and they're there to help, let's look at how exactly they can help you. Although your relationship counselor will have heard every kind of problem imaginable, they also realize that whatever you're going through is unique. They won't try to apply a blanket textbook solution, but instead will look to you for the solutions to your problems.

So, if you have to come up with all the answers, they can't really help anyway, right? Wrong! A counselor will certainly expect you to put effort into solving the issues that are souring your relationship yourselves, but he will work with you to do so.

A counselor will not judge you. He won't tell you what to do and won't persuade you to stay together if you would rather be apart. Counseling aims to help you improve your relationship and to ensure that you both develop a clear idea of what you want your future to be.

"Argument is the worst sort of communication."
JONATHAN SWIFT

Defining idea . . .

The counselor will guide you into finding out what lies at the root of your conflict and help you find ways to stop fighting. You'll be given a safe, neutral environment in which to work out exactly what it is you want from each other, and what you're willing to do to facilitate that happening. You'll be encouraged to find new ways to communicate, and shown how to avoid trigger points for argument.

What happens if this process reveals that divorce is the option you want? Surely counseling has been a failure? Not at all. You now know that your relationship is over, and you are both free to move on with your lives. Going through the counseling process to find this out may well have saved you countless arguments and a lot of heartache. All counseling services will offer you support as you separate and even after the divorce has gone through.

How did it go?

Q   How can counseling help me if my partner refuses to go?

A   *Simply go alone. Although not ideal, it will give you the opportunity to work through your own issues, and give you new ways to approach improving your relationship. Your partner may notice the changes and decide to go along, too. Phone and online services may be a nonthreatening way to encourage your spouse to participate.*

Q   How will we cope with the shame of seeing a counselor?

A   *There is no shame involved. You're being brave and responsible in seeking help, and this is praiseworthy, not shameful. Your consultations will be confidential and there's no reason anyone else need know about them.*

22

Don't do it like that— do it like this!

Why do other people think they know how to lead your life better than you do? And why do they insist on telling you? Remember, advice is there to be ignored—learn how to take on the good stuff and throw out the garbage.

Even though your friends and family may have your best intentions at heart, too much concern and advice can be a bad thing, especially when you're going through something as traumatic as a divorce. Suddenly everyone's an expert, and it's driving you mad.

BITE YOUR TONGUE OR BITE BACK?

Have you noticed how people tend to fall into three categories? There are ones who practice schadenfreude and actively delight in your misfortune. Then there are those who are always telling you that no matter how bad your situation is, there's

Here's an idea for you . . .

Now is the time to actively choose who you want to support you. Maybe you've always hated Cassandra and Clive, and they were your ex's friend's anyway. What better time to get rid of them! If you don't want to listen to their opinions, allow yourself to say so. Stop making duty telephone calls, don't respond to theirs, and give the extra time to the friends you trust and respect. I call this the "rosebush and secateurs" approach to friendship. In other words you have to prune back the dead and rotten friendships to let new healthy ones grow in their place.

someone worse off than you. And finally there are the real friends who support and help unconditionally, and these ones are very rare.

The first thing to do if you have friends who fall into the first two categories is not to take it personally. Most of their comments and advice will say far more about them than you. Honestly! Think about it: people who actually enjoy the drama of your divorce even when you are hating every minute of it obviously have issues of their own to sort out. If they revel in the bad news that the court has awarded costs against you again, then what does this say about them? Well, first it tells you that you'd be far better off without them. Second, it reveals a lack of sensitivity and perception that will always prevent them from maintaining close friendships.

The people who insist that you look on the bright side at all times usually mean well and, in their own way, are trying to help. But I know from experience that some days you don't even *want* to look at anything positively and just want to be allowed to feel glum. Whatever they say, it is okay to feel like that sometimes.

These people can also be a little competitive. They often like to feel that their situation is always worse than yours. You know the type—if you've got a headache, they've got a migraine; if you've got a migraine, they've got a brain tumor.

In all of these cases you need to step back from the situation and assess if you want to discuss your personal problems with friends like these. After all, if you feel more like strangling them than sharing with them, it's probably best to bite your tongue before you bite back at them and cause a fight.

Maybe you'd love some advice but your friends haven't stuck around to give it. IDEA 5, *Circle of friends*, will help you out.

Try another idea . . .

CARING ISN'T ALWAYS SHARING

If you're in the situation where everyone is giving you advice, then you're probably quite an open person who likes to share problems. This in itself is very healthy, but you must choose who you share with carefully.

Your marriage is an intimate relationship between two people, and even when it breaks down it is best to treat it with respect. For example, you may have separated from your partner but not yet decided on a divorce. If you tell all your friends that your guy is a brute or your girl's a terror, you could create an awkward situation for your partner and your friends if you then decide to get back together.

We all need to talk, but choose trustworthy people to talk to. This is easier to do than you think. Simply ask yourself one thing: Who never gossips? Once you've identified this person, then talk to her. It will then be highly unlikely that the intimate details of your divorce will circulate around your social group like chickenpox at a toddler's birthday party.

"Advice is like snow—the softer it falls the longer it dwells upon and the deeper it sinks in the mind."
SAMUEL TAYLOR COLERIDGE

Defining idea . . .

87

Another great tip for avoiding the tidal wave of advice is to erect some sandbags to stop it from getting through. So, when someone asks you if you want their opinion, simply say no. This doesn't have to be done rudely. You can thank your friend for the concern, but say you think it's best to try it your way first. If, however, the tsunami of advice is unstoppable, simply smile and nod occasionally but mentally tune out. They can say what they like, but there's no rule that says you must listen.

How did it go?

Q   How can I avoid advice if it's my mom who's giving it?

A   *This is a tricky one, but you can try two approaches. If you have a good relationship with your mom, gently explain that you're doing the best you can and you're trying things your way first. Tell her that if it doesn't work, then you'll definitely ask for her opinion. If it's hard to talk to your mom, then listen to her advice, thank her for it, and then just ignore it. Works like a charm!*

Q   How do I know whose advice to take?

A   *First of all remember that you don't have to take anyone's advice if you don't want to. If you do need some words of wisdom then think logically about who to ask. Who do you trust? Who has been through a similar situation? Who has a life or relationship you admire?*

23

Single supplement

Has your divorce been a long haul? Do you need a break without breaking the bank? Don't be scared that you can't work out exactly how much your single supplement will cost. Vacationing alone needn't be hell.

It's scary vacationing alone for the first time. You've gone on vacation as a couple for so many years that you're worried you'll start talking to the empty deck chair beside you out of habit. Who's to say that deck chair has to be empty? And, even if it is, going on vacation alone doesn't necessarily mean that you'll be lonely.

TAKING THE PLUNGE

If you're really unhappy with going away without company, first of all explore the potential for vacation companions. Do you have any family who'd like to go away with you? Or what about friends? With over one in two marriages breaking down,

Here's an idea for you . . .

Do your homework and avoid the sins of the single supplement. A little research on your part can ensure you pay little or no extra for traveling alone. Use the Internet and your local travel agent to track down the companies that pride themselves on offering fair deals to lone travelers. Singles companies provide a range of holidays for the solo traveler, and some package vacations are also beginning to get rid of supplements. Traveling on special-interest vacations can also avoid the supplement trap, as can traveling off season— www.singlestravelintl.com suggests tips for supplement-free cruising.

there's a high likelihood that you'll have a divorced or separated friend who's as desperate for a week in Waikiki, or Wales, as you are.

Still no one? Then explore the companies who arrange vacations for single people. These are often a good bet for the first time you travel alone. Supplements will usually be included in the cost of the vacation so there aren't any hidden extras. Many of these firms also organize welcome and orientation meetings, escorted travel, and plenty of day trips to keep you occupied.

Of course, if you want to go on a singles vacation in order to look for a new love, then this is perfectly possible. But don't worry that if you go solo your travel company will expect you to return as a couple. Simply check out the company's philosophy before you book. Your travel agent can help you with this if you feel a bit shy about asking.

It can be daunting choosing the right vacation for your first solo adventure, but treat it as just that—an adventure! Think about it: For the first time in years, you can choose a vacation that's totally right for you. If you like sunbathing, you can choose somewhere where you can veg out on a beach for two weeks without anyone nagging at you to sightsee. And if you love museums, why not book a culture-fest of a vacation and wander through galleries until your feet drop off? The world's your oyster, so stop worrying and start enjoying!

Not quite ready to holiday alone? Look at IDEA 42, *Spas, bars, and chocolate*, for some other ways to give yourself a treat.

Try another idea . . .

SINGLE FAMILY FUN

So, how do you cope if you're going away for the first time as a single parent? The thought that you're going to have to pack, travel, entertain, reassure, and rest with no backup can seem very daunting. But that doesn't have to be the case. With careful planning, you can ensure that your vacation with the children is just as much fun this year as it was last year with your partner. The fact is that it may well be better. After all, there's no chance that marital arguments will sour the vacation this year, is there?

The key to a good single-parent family vacation is in the preparation. It's unlikely that you'll be able to get a late bargain anyway as you're only traveling with one adult in the family. So instead of worrying about this, use it to your advantage and book well in advance. Booking ahead ensures a greater degree of choice of resort and hotel.

Set a budget you can afford—work out what you'll need for spending money and any hidden extras, and stick to it. All-inclusives are a great choice for the single parent, as everything you pay for will be up front. That way you can enjoy all the food, drink, and activities available without worrying about the hotel bill.

"The man who goes off alone can start today; but he who travels with another must wait till he is ready."
HENRY DAVID THOREAU

Defining idea . . .

Look specifically for resorts with children's programs or day care to make sure that your kids have playmates and you have some rest. With lots of activities offered it's unlikely that you or the kids will feel isolated or lonely.

How did it go?

Q   **How do I ensure my children and I both have a relaxing and fun time on vacation when they hate the idea of kids' clubs?**

A   *There are two ways you can do this. You can choose an activity vacation that you and the children will both enjoy. If you've gone through a difficult divorce, activities such as skiing, hiking, or sailing can provide excellent opportunities to bond as a family unit. Or, if activity vacations aren't for you, then team up with another family. That way the children will have company without being in a kids' club, and you'll have some adult conversation, too.*

Q   **How can I travel alone safely? I'm nervous as I've never been away alone before.**

A   *It's natural to feel nervous, and sensible to be aware of safety issues. Simply follow all the precautions you would take at home, such as not walking alone late at night and using recommended taxi services. Travel with a tour group—either especially for singles, or simply a reliable package company with a representative on hand to turn to if you have difficulties. Choose your resort carefully and team up with another single on the holiday or even a friendly couple.*

24

Accentuate the positive, eliminate the negative

After years with the same partner, we all start believing the negative things they have told us about ourselves. Using affirming techniques and NLP, you can start to really believe in a new you.

Why is it easier to believe in the bad things than the good? Why do we put ourselves down? And why is it that if we say good things about ourselves we're perceived as being arrogant?

THE POWER OF POSITIVE

Unfortunately we seemingly accept negative comments and feelings much more easily than we do positive ones. Our confidence can be a fragile thing and if we have spent a number of years in a relationship with someone who accentuates our negative qualities, then it can take a real bashing.

Here's an idea for you . . .

Draw up a list of five positive affirmations and stick them in various places at home or at work. Post-it notes on your fridge, your desk, or a mirror can be a great way to remind you to be positive. Also try computer screensavers with your affirmations or positive images. Read your affirmations frequently and say them out loud as soon as you get up in the morning and whenever you can throughout the day. Keep the affirmations short, and focus on one to three areas that you'd like to improve. Some suggestions include: *I am calm, confident, and in control*; *I am attractive and vibrant*; *I am worthy of success*; *I am generous, good, and kind*; *I am happy and strong*.

Divorce can also batter our confidence, especially if it has cost a lost of time, money, and heartache. We can feel very low and our confidence is often at rock bottom. However, with time and care our self-esteem can be nurtured back to health, even after a long and destructive marriage.

Although it's a sad fact that many marriages are ending in divorce, the upside to this is that there is a growing understanding of the effects it has on the individuals concerned and there's far more help available to assist you with post-divorce recovery.

NEURO-LINGUISTIC PROGRAMMING (NLP)

Don't worry, this isn't some kind of secret government brainwashing initiative. Neuro-linguistic programming is simply a model of communication. It helps you to communicate more effectively with yourself and with others.

First, let's look at what NLP really means. As with all things, it's much easier to understand when it's broken down into bite-size chunks. *Neuro* refers to our neurological processes. These are the processes our brain uses to make sense of the world, and are quite literally our senses of sight, hearing, touch, taste, and smell.

Neurology covers all things brain-related and deals with our thought processes as well as our physiological reactions. *Linguistic* simply means language. We use language to communicate with each other and to express our thoughts and feelings. *Programming* refers to the way in which we organize our thoughts. Just like computers are programmed to respond to certain commands, so too are our brains.

NLP looks at the way we process everything that we think and feel. It looks at our reactions to our experiences and how we use language to describe them. In essence, the way it works is very simple. Think of it this way: Programming is simply training. NLP aims to train us to think and respond positively and to eliminate negative patterns of thought, expression, and response.

If you're always told by your partner that you have fat legs, you will begin to believe it, even if originally you thought your legs were as slim as reeds. Why is that? Your legs aren't fat, but you believe they are. The answer is that your partner has created a strong thought association in your head—legs and fat. These negative patterns can develop without you even realizing it.

The first thing you need to do to change the pattern is start to be actively aware of the negative things you or your partner says or has said. For example, do you often start sentences with "I'm sure I'm wrong . . ." or "I know Sheila/Bill always told me I was bad at . . ."? If you do, then the negative patterns of behavior and belief are active in your daily language.

All's going well, but still have a few flabby parts? Take a look at IDEA 25, *Body beautiful*, and learn to love your body.

Try another idea . . .

"No one can make you feel inferior without your consent."
ELEANOR ROOSEVELT

Defining idea . . .

95

It's a lot easier to get rid of them once you know they are there. Start writing down all these negative things and every time you hear yourself say one, immediately stop and replace it with a more positive comment. Even if you're just thinking negative thoughts, stop and say something positive out loud. Quickly get into a pattern with this, and positive responses will come much more naturally than they did to start with. Soon your negative vocabulary will be eradicated entirely.

How did it go?

Q   How can I change into a positive person when I've felt negatively about myself for so long?

A   *Simply start slowly and do a little at a time. First, decide that you really want to change into a positive person; just making this decision will change the way you view things. Focus on one aspect at a time. For example, examine the way you feel about your appearance and write some affirmations about that. Then move on to aspects of your work life, and your relationship with friends and family. Little by little you'll start to feel much more positive.*

Q   How can I use affirmations when I can't think of one positive thing to say about myself?

A   *Ask someone you trust who is always really positive about you to help. Get them to write down some positive things and then work them up into affirmations using your own words. Once you start to notice a few good things about yourself, more will follow.*

25

Body beautiful

After diving under the covers with the same partner for years, your body image may need some work after the divorce. You need to start respecting and enjoying your body again—even the flabby parts.

It's easy to forget that our bodies are incredible, especially when they start to sag a bit or soften up. Just remember: your body may not be perfect, but it can be a shining reflection of the person inside, and it can give you an awful lot of fun.

THE HANGOVER

As we all know, a hangover is a horrible thing. The indulgences of the night before come back to haunt us, and we suffer all the way. Similarly, our negative body image is always to do with the way we've been treated before. It's a hangover from all the negative comments from our partners, parents, and friends. And it can also be—just like a hangover—self-inflicted. But also just like a hangover, a negative body image

Here's an idea for you . . .

So, you're going to bed with someone new for the first time. Are you worried you'll be embarrassed by your flabby parts? Well don't be. Use some camouflage. Plan soft lighting and flattering yet concealing underwear. Great scent can be a great disguise. Use camouflaging positions, too. If you've got a great bum, backward is best. If you've got a beer belly get her on top so your tummy won't hang down. Chances are you'll have shared a kiss and a canoodle or two before this stage, so they'll know about your chunky tummy or smaller than average boobs already.

is temporary. It may stick around for a while, but it will eventually fade and be forgotten.

Divorce can really take its toll on your body image. If you've discovered that your spouse has had an affair, it can blow holes in your confidence. You immediately start comparing yourself—was he taller than I? Are her boobs bigger than mine? I suppose size really does matter! You know the routine.

Even if there wasn't an affair, perhaps you've been in a sexless marriage for years, and body image is only about how the car looks? Whatever the reasons behind the breakup, it's likely that your body image will have been damaged. And this can be a particular problem when you move on to a new relationship.

TIME TO TURN THE LIGHT ON

The first time we move into a new physical relationship after a marriage can be terrifying. You've probably been used to wearing your granny panties, Spiderman pajamas, and taking a hot drink to bed. But now, for the first time in ages, you're taking a hot date to bed instead and you're scared.

The last time someone paid you a compliment you had a spiral perm or a mullet, so how will your new bed partner respond to your body? The trick is to think confidently! There's nothing more sexy than someone who feels sexy and attractive themselves. They ooze confidence and pump out pheromones until you feel drunk. So why not join the party?

Positive thinking is the key to a good self-image. Look at IDEA 24, *Accentuate the positive, eliminate the negative*, and perfect yours.

Try another idea . . .

Think about the parts of your body you like. Dress to impress, and show off what you've got. Capri trousers or high-heeled shoes will make the most of delicate female ankles, and guys, a crisp white shirt rolled up to reveal tanned muscular forearms will make girls melt.

Instead of seeing the flabby parts of your body as a problem, look at them as a challenge. Set yourself goals to lose weight and eat more healthily. Buy upbeat music or treat yourself to a massage if you've achieved something rather than rewarding yourself with food. And exercise the fun way—if you hate the gym, try Rollerblading instead.

Challenge yourself to focus on your good points as well as just the bad. Girls, so what if you've got some stretch marks? You got them from having your children, so be proud and see them as part of your history. Guys, maybe you've got a few more lines around your eyes after the divorce. See them as craggy and showing character, and a sign that you've got through tough times.

"You don't love a woman because she is beautiful. She is beautiful because you love her."
MODERN SLOGAN

Defining idea . . .

Don't look at women's and men's magazines and get depressed by the cover girl/guy. Instead, take on board the tips inside (and remember that the pictures are airbrushed to perfection anyway!). Magazines are stuffed full of advice about how to make the ordinary seem extraordinary, so use it. Men, get a back wax and feel silky smooth. Women, have your eyebrows shaped and let your eyes smolder.

Try changing your environment as well as your body. Turn your bedroom into a boudoir to make you feel sexy, or paint the walls of your sitting room in bright jazzy colors that feel vibrant and alive.

How did it go?

Q   How can I continue to make the best of myself? I've been a gym junkie but I still think I look chunky.

A   *Work on improving your posture. Stand up tall with shoulders back, tummy in, and neck straight. This will take at least three pounds off the way you look, and holding yourself like this will tighten your abs, too.*

Q   How can I believe my new partner when he says I'm sexy? My ex never said I was sexy.

A   *Forget your ex! Concentrate on what your new partner is saying and believe in the present not the past. Instead of just telling you what parts of your body he likes, get your partner to kiss and caress them until you surrender and believe him.*

26

"And guest" is positive

The invitation drops through the door, and for the first time it doesn't have Mr. & Mrs. on the front. Instead it's just your name, "and guest." Don't refuse invitations because you're on your own. Plunder the positive possibilities of "and guest"!

Just think of all the grim socializing you did with your ex: the boring cocktail parties his boss threw every Christmas, the double dates you had to go on with her dreadful best friend, and the torture of his family gatherings. Well let me be the first to tell you the good news—you never have to go again!

TAKE A DEEP BREATH

So why is it that when you get an invitation for you, and guest, to attend a special bash you suddenly feel depressed? This is actually a perfectly normal reaction. For

Here's an idea for you . . .

Been invited out? Then beat your nerves with preparation. If you are a little scared about socializing again, especially on your own, take some fail-safe precautions. Find out exactly what the dress code is and try on your outfit before the event. Plan how you'll get there and back, and book a taxi in advance if necessary. If you're worried you'll get tongue tied, plan some things to talk about. Look at a newspaper or magazine for neutral topics, and ask lots of friendly questions. If you're sensitive about your divorce, rehearse what to say if you're asked about it.

all the years of your marriage, you and your ex were a unit. If you received an invitation, it was invariably to both of you, and now it's not. There's a security that comes from going somewhere as a couple and it can be scary the first few times you go somewhere on your own.

Just about everyone feels this way after a divorce. Some of us are relieved that we can be single and ourselves again, others are deeply sad that they are no longer part of a couple, and some feel a mixture of both.

However you feel, when that invitation to you and guest falls on the doormat, that's the time to take a deep breath, gather your courage, and go!

A BREATH OF FRESH AIR

Once you've taken that deep breath, you may well be surprised to find that you've gulped in a great lungful of fresh air, and it feels really good. Think of all the new opportunities that are in front of you. For the first time in ages you can attend a social event exactly as you want to. If you want to take someone with you then you can, and if you want to go alone, then that's fine, too.

If you go alone you have a wonderful opportunity to meet new people at the event. This is especially true at parties and weddings. You may think that everyone will be in couples at a wedding, but this isn't the case at all. The bride and groom are bound to have single friends—after all, up until that day they were single themselves. And it's well known that many people find their life partners at weddings.

Need a date? Why not give online dating a try? Look at IDEA 4, *Online is divine*, and get started.

Try another idea . . .

If you don't want to go alone, there are lots of other options. If you're at the right stage emotionally, why not ask a date? Perhaps it could be the ideal opportunity to introduce your new girl/boyfriend to your friends. Or maybe you could go with a friend and simply have a good laugh. Maybe you could even take your mom, dad, son, or daughter and make it a family event.

It's normal to feel scared when you're getting back into a social scene again after a divorce. You're bound to feel sensitive and a little scared of the new territory in front of you. But just remember that you are in control of the situation.

You can pick and choose the events you go to, so start slowly if need be. For example, maybe you won't feel comfortable attending a dinner party full of couples, or being given a blind date to hook up with. But perhaps you would feel happy at a party where there was a good mix of singles and marrieds of all ages. Choose wisely, and if necessary, do a little homework on who will be there.

"Now I can wear heels!"
NICOLE KIDMAN, on divorcing Tom Cruise

Defining idea . . .

Be confident and look forward to the event. Treat yourself to a new party shirt or a pair of killer heels. Spray yourself liberally with something yummy, do your hair, and have some fun. This is your opportunity to show that you are getting over the divorce and it hasn't gotten you down. You can signal that you're moving on, you're enjoying life, and you're not to be pitied. Social events like this can really boost your confidence, so grab them with both hands.

How did it go?

Q   Should I go to a friend's baby's christening if my ex is there, too?

A   *Well how do you feel about it? If you're comfortable going, then go. Of course, remember that the event isn't about you and your ex, so don't cause any tension. Simply avoid him if you can. If you feel uncomfortable attending, then explain to your friend how you feel and ask for her advice.*

Q   Is it really okay to take my mom along as my "and guest"?

A   *Why not? If you've been given an open invitation to an event, then you're free to bring anyone you choose. Just check the event's suitable for you and your mom—she may love a trip to the races, but might not feel so comfortable in a strip joint. A courtesy would be to let the person who invited you know who you'll be bringing and then they'll be prepared for your guest.*

27

Staying strong

Mental health isn't all about a stiff upper lip. Physical fitness, diet, and exercise are all part of staying on top of the situation. Caring for your body while your mind is in turmoil is essential. Here's how.

Keeping fit has many meanings, all of which are relevant if you're going through a divorce. This idea takes you through the key steps in staying strong.

KEEP FIT

Of course, it's essential to exercise and keep yourself physically fit. Exercise releases endorphins, which help to raise your mood and to fend off depression, so the more you can do the better. Keeping fit will also help you maintain a good body image. If you're looking after your body, toning, and exercising it, you're far less likely to feel unattractive—a common side effect of separation and divorce.

So, what can you do if you're not a natural gym bunny and you think a Swiss Ball is a new kind of cocktail? Well, there are plenty of alternatives. Simply walking whenever you can is a great way of toning up and burning off a few calories. Get

Here's an idea for you . . .

Give yourself a stress test!

1. **Are you more tired than normal, sleeping later or napping in the afternoons?**
2. **Are you irritable and easy to anger?**
3. **Have you broken out in spots or an itchy rash?**
4. **Is your hair dull, lank, or falling out?**
5. **Have you bitten your nails?**
6. **Have you increased your levels of drinking or smoking?**

If you've answered yes to three or more of these questions, it's likely your stress levels are high. Start doing regular deep breathing exercises to lower your pulse and blood pressure. Enroll in yoga classes if you feel it hard to do on your own. Look at your diet, too, and eliminate salt, sugar, and saturated fats and take a good multivitamin supplement daily. This will all help to bring your stress levels down.

off the bus one stop earlier, or walk the children to school. Climb the stairs in the office rather than using the elevator and walk out to get your sandwiches rather than ordering in. Too boring? Try salsa dancing classes—as well as burning off calories and toning your muscles, you might bump into somebody special.

If you are into the gym thing, then great! Work with a qualified instructor to create a program that's good for you. Set realistic goals and have a short program and a longer one. That way you can just pop in when you've only got a small amount of time and still achieve something. Gyms are also great for meeting people and having some "you" time. If childcare is a problem then choose a gym with day care. If you're pushed for time, why not join a gym close to work and go on your lunch hour?

NOURISH YOURSELF

Stress affects our health enormously, and divorce is one of the most stressful experiences we can go through. When we are in a stressful situation—say, for example, an argument with the ex about maintenance payments—our brains recognize this and create a physical "fight or flight" response. In the days of early man this was particularly useful if confronting a woolly mammoth, but it can cause us problems if we're trying to have a rational discussion.

Stressed? Exhausted? Need a vacation? Check out IDEA 23, *Single supplement*, and get packing.

Try another idea . . .

The "fight or flight" reaction causes our heart rate and blood pressure to rise, and our bodies start producing huge quantities of adrenaline. Now, adrenaline's a really useful chemical when outrunning that woolly mammoth, but if you're stressed over a long period of time it can affect your health.

There are lots of things you can do to look after your adrenal glands. First of all begin to take a vitamin B complex, because when we're under pressure our bodies tend to gobble these vital vits like a sports car does gas. Our adrenal glands are aggravated by stimulants such as caffeine, so cut out the coffee and drink herbal tea instead. Avoid sugary foods and especially salt, as they will all make matters worse.

Try to eat "super foods" such as broccoli, beans, and lentils as well as fruits rich in potassium such as bananas. And don't forget your oily fish! Adding even a few of these foods to your daily diet will dramatically improve your vitamin and mineral levels.

"You don't get ulcers from what you eat; you get them from what's eating you."
VICKI BAUM, novelist

Defining idea . . .

Keep a look out for symptoms of tiredness, indigestion, and headache—all symptoms of stress—and consult a clinical nutritionist if you feel you need help with your diet.

It's easy to forget to care for ourselves during stressful periods in our lives, but taking a few easy steps toward nourishing our bodies will help us nourish our minds, too.

How did it go?

Q   How can I do any exercise when I'm so exhausted by my divorce that I have no energy?

A   *I know it seems impossible, but a little gentle exercise will boost your energy levels. Start with walking more briskly than usual and gradually build up to something more energetic. Look at your diet, too. Is it full of sugars and refined foods? These can sap your energy and make you feel tired. Look to nuts and fruit as snacks and eat little meals often.*

Q   How can I join a gym when the divorce is costing me every penny I have?

A   *Rather than choosing a posh private gym, why not look at what your local YMCA has to offer? The gyms can be just as well-equipped as private ones, and cost less. Or, if it's viable for you, look at off-peak membership and periods when the joining fee is reduced.*

28

Dividing the spoils

Although not usually as financially imperative as dividing the house or the bank account, dividing up your personal possessions can be difficult and emotional. After all, can you remember who owned the lava lamp and who bought the first Duran Duran album? This idea will show you how to cope if you can't.

So you're standing in the family home looking at the huge number of possessions you've acquired over the years and your stomach's sinking quicker than the *Titanic*. Where on earth do you start?

LISTS, LISTS, AND MORE LISTS

Bet you never even knew you had so much stuff! But then you did forget about the loft, the spare room, the closet under the stairs, and the shed, didn't you? Before you give up and decide that the minimalist look is just what you want for your new life, take a deep breath, grab a pen and paper, and start to make a list.

Here's an
idea for
you . . .

If things are acrimonious between you, it's unlikely that you'll want to do each other any favors when it comes to dividing the spoils. You need the tactics of an expert negotiator. If you're a little bit sneaky you should be able to get exactly what you want. Simply pick an item that you know your partner will want, but that you have no desire to keep, and pretend you're desperate for it. Weep and wail if necessary and declare undying love for his collection of antique toenail clippers. Then give in gracefully, but only on the condition that you get the item you really covet.

Start by listing everything you own as a comprehensive inventory and then divide it into subsections. Note down all your personal possessions, such as jewelry and items that have been given to you individually as gifts. Then make a list of what you absolutely must have, what you'd like but could negotiate on, and what you don't want at all. Make sure that this last list is for your eyes only and that your ex doesn't take a sneaky peek. This will allow you greater room for negotiating later.

The next thing to do is arrange a mutually convenient time with your partner and go through the house and the inventory together. If relations are particularly strained between you, consider bringing a mutual friend along who has both of your interests at heart and can help you stay rational.

Once you've come to a mutual agreement about the division of your possessions, write it down. Keep one copy each and sign them both. As soon as you've done this, get the agreement legalized by an attorney and made part of your official separation and divorce.

Of course, you may find that there's just no way to agree on who gets what, and things may start to get heated. That's the time to get some extra help. Start with a mediation service specially trained to help you reach mutually acceptable agreements on issues like these. If you're still getting nowhere, then hand everything over to your attorneys and let the court decide.

You've done the possessions but who gets the house? Have a look at IDEA 36, *Your place or mine?*, for advice.

Try another idea . . .

EMOTIONAL ECHOES

It all sounds straightforward and practical doesn't it? Unfortunately when you actually come to dividing up everything you've owned together and enjoyed or hated over the years, it doesn't feel so easy. In fact it can be heartbreaking. So how do you cope?

First, recognize that this may be one of the hardest parts of your divorce and prepare yourself for the feelings of sadness that may come, too. It's perfectly natural to get upset about splitting your things down the middle. Possessions may just be material things, but they can symbolize happy and sad times, with all the memories and echoes.

Prepare for these feelings by doing as much as you can on your own before you get together with your partner for the final decisions. That way if you end up in floods of unmanly tears over the picture you bought in Greece on your honeymoon, or start to sniffle over the silverware, then your spouse won't see. If you do get upset when your partner's there, then don't feel bad about it. Simply ask for a bit of time out and allow yourself space to recover before moving on.

"Money talks but all mine ever says is good-bye!"
ANONYMOUS

Defining idea . . .

111

It's also useful to recognize where the emotional triggers might lie. For example, have you thought about how you'll divide up all your photos? This is often a tricky one, but the "one for me and one for you" approach really does work. Simply go through every album and deal them out one by one. That way a fair distribution will be reached. It's cheaper than having everything copied and quicker than trying to reach an agreement on each one. If, however, you never want to see your partner again, the photo issue will be less pressing. Maybe you could just take turns with the scissors!

How did it go?

Q How can I stop my husband from getting everything? He's as hard as nails and never compromises.

A *First of all remind him that you are entitled by law to a percentage of your possessions no matter what he says. Second, think positively and try to negotiate with him logically. If this doesn't work, contact a mediator for some practical help. Of course, if your husband is abusive in any way, deal with everything through your lawyer.*

Q Is it fair that my wife gets more than half of our possessions?

A *Unfortunately the question of fairness is subjective. If the majority of your possessions were hers before the marriage, then they will probably return to her when the marriage dissolves. Also, if she is going to have less in terms of cash than you, then perhaps she will get more possessions instead. If you're worried, contact an attorney for advice.*

29

The green-eyed monster

Even if you're happy about being divorced or were the one to instigate proceedings, it can come as a bit of a shock when you find out that your ex is seeing someone else. This idea offers ways to handle it when your ex gets a new you.

Usually after the shock passes you'll smart a little for a while and then get back to the main business at hand—focusing on your own life. But what happens if it doesn't work that way and rather than feeling just a little sore, you're seething with jealousy?

JUST A BIT JEALOUS?

Somehow you always thought that you'd be the first one to find someone new. Now you've heard that your ex has done it first and is mooning around like a love-struck teenager. Not that you're bothered, of course! So why have your eyes turned a bright shade of emerald green? It's true that jealousy really can be a beast within. To

Here's an idea for you . . .

If you've just found out your former partner has found someone new, it's impossible not to compare yourself to that person. But the idea here is to make that comparison a positive one, one that is entirely in your favor. Don't look at all the attributes the new guy or girl has that make you feel insecure. Instead, literally write down the comparisons that make you feel good. So what if he's got a degree in astrophysics from MIT—can he bench press 200 pounds, like you? If you're having problems doing this, invite your bitchiest friend over and get her to help you with your list. You'll be amazed at how good you feel when you're done.

make sure it doesn't take over your life, you need to work out why you're feeling like this.

What exactly are you jealous of? Perhaps you feel that your ex has moved on and you've been left behind. Even if it seems that way, you need to remember that lives move at different paces. You might not be ready for a new relationship yet and are taking the sensible approach of having some time just for you first.

Perhaps you're just jealous of the fact that your ex has found some companionship? The months after divorce can feel very lonely when you've been used to the closeness that comes with a marriage. Even if it was an unhappy marriage, there is a security that stems from sharing a home with someone and interacting with that person on a daily basis. So, be kind to yourself and give yourself time to get over it.

TAMING THE GREEN-EYED MONSTER

Jealousy is often a sign of unresolved anger or grief and may occur because you haven't yet been able to come to terms with the breakdown of your marriage. The key word here is "yet." Perhaps you didn't want the divorce in the first place, or were still in love with your spouse even though you separated. If this is the case, then any feelings of love or rejection you've repressed will jump up and demand attention when you see or hear that your ex has found someone new. Again this is a natural reaction to have, and once you've recognized this, it will be a lot easier to deal with.

You're divorced, so you know the relationship is over. Now it's a matter of moving on in the most positive way possible. This doesn't mean you should ignore your feelings of jealousy. Far from it, they should be acknowledged and allowed to come out. After all, jealousy is a natural emotion, but a negative one.

Try to make these feelings work for you rather than against you. Don't deny how you feel, but deal with it. Jealousy is often a result of insecurity and divorce is the master when it comes to making us feel insecure.

Work on ways of building your self-esteem. Treat yourself to that course of personal training at the gym that you've always wanted, or improve the skill sets you already have. Play to your strengths and drown out the voice of insecurity that fuels your jealousy and ask yourself whether you are really hurt, or was it just a blow to your pride?

Can you move from mating for life to being just friends? Have a look at IDEA 40, *Staying friends*, to see if you can.

Try another idea . . .

"Anger and jealousy can no more bear to lose sight of their objects than love."
GEORGE ELIOT

Defining idea . . .

115

How did it go?

Q   How can I cope with my jealousy when all I want to do is phone my ex's new girlfriend and tell her exactly what he's like?

A   *A desire for revenge is often a side effect of jealousy, but don't give in to such negative emotions. Turning your jealous feelings into jealous actions will only hurt you. If you give in to your desire to call her, it's you who will look bad. Relations between the three of you will become very unpleasant and this could have severe ramifications if there are children or mutual friends involved. Use anger management techniques and phone a friend to vent your feelings instead of calling her.*

Q   How can I ensure my children aren't affected by my jealousy of my ex-wife's new husband?

A   *Focusing your feelings entirely on their needs will help enormously. They will have gone through enough trauma with the divorce, so don't add to it. Make sure you don't talk negatively about their new stepfather, and don't go along with negative statements about the new family setup. You will always be their dad, so tell them this and constantly reinforce your love for them.*

30

Not so young, free, and single

Will you be celebrating your silver wedding anniversary or is the silvery glow of your relationship well and truly tarnished? Here's how to cope if the party is definitely off.

Are you a member of the "baby boomer breakup" generation? Are you being accused of a midlife crisis? You're not alone—there's an increasing number of couples divorcing after twenty-five years of marriage or more.

BYE-BYE, BABY . . .

The optimism and hope that filled the hearts of the survivors of the Second World War also filled the maternity wards. The "baby boom," as it came to be known, repopulated a world decimated by the tragedy of war.

Two of these children grew up to be my parents and, like many of their generation, they married young and had their own children in the early optimism of their

Here's an idea for you . . .

If you're living in the shadow of your past life, turn the spotlight on the new one. To do this, a simple visualization technique can be used. First, think of positive aspects of your new life—the place you live, the people you've met, and the activities you can now do. Then take some quiet time, close your eyes, and visualize these new things. Then gradually intensify all the colors. Brighten everything until details and colors glow and shine brightly in your mind. Do this every day and you'll soon feel positive about your new life and your future.

twenties. There was no way I could tell at the celebration of their silver wedding anniversary that the following year they would be separated.

As I talked to more people I was surprised to discover that my parents weren't unusual in their "baby boomer breakup." Divorce isn't restricted to any age group. Marriages can fail at any time and it seems the danger point is no longer occurring with the "seven year itch." In fact it's the "twenty-seven year itch" that has the couple concerned clawing each other's eyes out.

So why leave it so late to get divorced? Surely by that stage in a relationship you will have ironed out the creases or at least found ways to live with them? Of course, it's true that many couples decide to stay together even though they have problems. If they get along together well enough then why should they put themselves through the trauma of a divorce? That attitude may work for some people, but it's growing as outmoded as woodchip wallpaper.

As people are living longer and remaining healthy and sexually active well into their eighties, why should they give up on love and happiness in their fifties? Okay, fair enough, but what about taking the children into consideration? Well, the baby boomer breakup generation have done exactly that and considered their children often above their own needs for many years. My research has shown that many couples divorcing after their twenty-fifth wedding anniversary responsibly waited for their children to finish their education before splitting up, minimizing the trauma caused.

Are your parents going through a breakup? Take a look at IDEA 31, *You can't get divorced, you're my parents!*, for advice.

Try another idea . . .

BOOM TIME!

Of course, divorcing later in life does bring its own set of problems. Many people splitting with their spouses after decades will feel the loneliness of being single acutely. It may take longer to come to terms with the end of a long marriage than a short one and it may take some time to build up the courage to date again. However, people who divorce in their fifties can conversely have the best of the situation.

Think about it. By the time you have reached your fifties your finances are likely to be healthy and stable, your family is probably grown and engrossed in their own lives, and your life experience will have equipped you for dealing with all sorts of situations. These are all factors that can be turned to your advantage.

Maybe you were used to living in a four-bedroom house in the suburbs, complete with double garage, but do you really need that now? Although you may be sad to leave your family home, think of the excitement of having something just for you after all these years. You can choose where and how you live and focus on your needs rather than those of a spouse or family.

"Life begins at forty!"
MODERN PROVERB

Defining idea . . .

Many people divorcing later in life use their newfound freedom to indulge in passions that married and family life has necessitated be put on hold. The number of older people taking singles vacations and even adventure breaks is growing every year. Far from divorcées in their fifties sitting at home and ruing what might have been, they are grabbing life by the scruff of the neck and giving it a good shake.

How did it go?

Q   How can I enjoy my new life when my wife has taken half of everything I've got?

A   *Stop focusing on the negative. You may have lost half, but you still have half. Provided your children have been accounted for in the settlement, you only have your needs to focus on. Start thinking in a different way. For example, you may live somewhere smaller but treat it as a bachelor pad. You may not have the SUV anymore, but why not buy something small and nippy?*

Q   How can I see my future positively? I'm a fifty-year-old woman with no skills other than being a wife and mother.

A   *First of all, recognize that there are hundreds of skills involved in being a wife and a mother. Second, use this opportunity to learn new skills and focus on you. And third, remember that many companies are eager for mature staff with life skills rather than simply qualifications.*

31

You can't get divorced, you're my parents!

Whether you're fourteen or forty, your parents' divorce can throw your world upside down. You'll need to find ways to get your world the right way up again.

Many grown-up children find it hard to accept their parents as regular people. But when parents divorce, children are forced to see them in a different light and this can unleash a powerful cocktail of feelings.

EMOTIONAL RAINBOW

Whatever age you are, when you discover your parents are getting divorced you are bound to go through a whole rainbow of feelings. Shock, relief, fear, anger, sadness, and worry are all common emotions, but perhaps the most common of all is guilt.

Here's an idea for you . . .

Quit being a child of divorce. You are the child of your parents, not the offspring of their divorce. It's important to realize this distinction so you can move on from the legacy of their divorce. So rather than seeing your parents' divorce as negative, instead see that it may give you a chance to avoid making the same mistakes they did. Be aware you may be sensitive to issues like infidelity or jealousy because it ruined your parents' marriage. Use this awareness positively—tell your partner you feel strongly about these issues and that you know they will be a hot spot for you. Look for positive images of marriage and talk to friends or family who have happy and long-term marriages to reinforce it as a positive state in your own mind.

No matter what the reasons behind our parents' split, it's not unusual to feel we are in some way responsible. That's when the guilt kicks in. Maybe we caused them too much trouble. Maybe we didn't allow them enough time for each other. And even if it wasn't directly our fault, maybe there was something we could have done to prevent it.

We always feel we are at the center of our parents' lives, and of course we are to a great extent. But we aren't the *only* thing in their lives. Our parents will have reasons entirely of their own for getting divorced, none of which will have anything to do with us. Realizing this is central to getting rid of our guilt.

Perhaps you feel that your parents are so focused on their divorce that you are overlooked. It's common to feel that your parents are making you take a backseat to their own troubles, but give them time. Let them deal with this trauma in their lives first. They're still there for you, they just need to shift their own focus for a while.

You may also get caught up being the peacemaker between your parents. This is an unhealthy role for a child of any age to have and you need to avoid it before you become a casualty of the war. Remember, this is their divorce, not yours, and they must deal with it between themselves.

Part of a baby boomer breakup? Look at IDEA 30, *Not so young, free, and single*, and you'll be glad to find you're not alone.

Try another idea . . .

CAUGHT IN THE CROSSFIRE

When your parents' marriage becomes a war zone, it's not always easy to avoid the barrage of bitterness that they may fire at each other. Your parents may try to make you take sides. Don't. Whatever they feel for each other, you have a right to a loving relationship with each parent. Taking sides may severely damage your relationship with one parent and could be a decision you regret later. You don't deserve to be in the middle, so tell them so.

Although your parents are understandably caught up in the drama of their divorce, you have a right to whatever feelings pop up along the way. Talk about them and deal with them as they arise. If you can't do this with your parents, do so with other family or friends. Draw strength from others and share the burden.

"Few parents nowadays pay any regard to what their children say to them. The old-fashioned respect for the young is dying out."
OSCAR WILDE

Defining idea . . .

You still have a right to be a significant part of your family whether your parents are divorced or not. Of course things will change. Living arrangements, family events, and new partners can cause upheaval, but you are still entitled to care and concern. If you feel you aren't getting this, then vocalize your feelings in a sensitive and logical way.

Sometimes the scariest fear of all can be the unknown, so inform yourself about your parents' divorce. Find out exactly what will go on and remove the threat of any nasty surprises. That way, if your parents ask you for advice you can also be informed and calm in your answer.

Divorce affects entire families, so don't be scared of sharing your feelings with your close relatives or extended family. Being prepared, informed, and aware can make this experience a whole lot better.

Q **How can I believe the divorce isn't my problem when my mom is always telling me it is?**

How did it go?

A *It's hard to accept, but the divorce really isn't your fault. Your mom is using you as an excuse not to face the real reasons behind the split. Refuse to discuss your so-called "responsibility" with your mother and end the conversation calmly but firmly. If appropriate, discuss your fears with siblings or other family members and get one of them to talk to your mom on your behalf.*

Q **How can I stop my parents from depending on me for total emotional support?**

A *Calmly explain to them that while you are more than willing to help them through the divorce, you cannot be the main source of support. Explain that it puts you in a difficult situation as you feel your loyalties are split and that you also need time for your own feelings. Encourage them to talk to others; in turn, share your problem with other family members or friends.*

32

The wicked stepparent

Nearly a quarter of kids in the US live in stepfamilies, so it really is time to move on from the fairy-tale image of the wicked stepparent. Stop expecting to live in that role; you *can* banish the nightmares.

Love me, love my kids . . . Do you feel more like the wicked witch than the blushing bride? Or maybe you're planning an audition for the Child Catcher in Chitty Chitty Bang Bang. You don't have to.

Divorce is increasingly common the world over and so is remarriage. As our perception of family shifts, so should our perception of the role and importance of a stepparent. After the trauma of a divorce, the stepparent can provide stability and continuity for any children involved.

Of course, being a stepfamily is never easy, but it seems to me that we forget that rifts, tensions, and feuds can occur just as easily within a biological family. There will, however, be different tensions within a stepfamily so being prepared and informed about what these may be provides a head start on creating a happy family life.

Here's an idea for you . . .

Be their friend. I've found this is the best way to cope when you find yourself the stepparent of teenagers. Your stepchildren will need reassurance that you have no wish to replace their parent but they'll also need to know that you want to have them in your life. Try to *show* as well as *tell* them this. So, try taking part in stuff they're interested in, but in a different way from their biological parent. If Dad always takes them to football games, arrange to watch a game on TV to show you're interested but not taking over. Let them call you by your name, and if they suggest using "Mom" or "Dad" later you'll know it's a decision they're happy with.

BLEND IT LIKE THE BRADYS!

The biggest problem for the stepfamily is often torn loyalties. When children are integrated into a new family after divorce they may feel less important than they were in the biological family. They can feel the parent who has remarried is being disloyal to their ex-spouse and the stepparent is responsible for that. The newlyweds will, of course, want to prioritize each other, but a situation of "new spouse versus biological family" unit ultimately results in conflict.

"Why did you have to marry X? We were so much better off when it was just us" is a familiar cry to the parent who has just remarried. So is the phrase, "Why do you always have to put your children before me?" from the new spouse. Quite simply, no one wants to lose out on love. Care, time, and commitment can ensure that nobody does.

In an attempt to move away from "step," the term "blended family" has been coined. Don't think this means a quick blender-style mix; instead, try to think of it as the slow-cooker approach to creating a family. Expecting to cook up a stepfamily as quickly as you would a microwave meal is a recipe for disaster. Placing everything in a large pot with lots of room to move, a very gentle heat, and giving it plenty of time to cook will ensure the hard barriers break down and the flavors blend perfectly.

Check out IDEA 34, *Second time around*, for more tips on remarriage.

Try another idea . . .

So, don't expect anything to happen instantly. Getting to know anyone takes time, and getting to know your stepchildren takes longer. Remarriage can be seen by children as nothing but a loss. They've lost the hope that their parents will ever get back together, and they've lost the total attention from their parent. Your role is to gradually change this perception and show them that they've gained—because they now have you and maybe new siblings, too.

You first need to accept that your new partner and their children come as a package. The trick here is to gently become part of the bonds that tie the package together.

Even if your stepchildren liked you when you were dating their parent, they may now feel threatened by you in your new role as husband or wife. Try to reassure them with actions as well as words. Allow them time alone with their parent, and also with you, to show them how special they are to both of you. Maybe even discuss what role you are expected to play by talking it through with your new spouse and his children.

"Love has nothing to do with what you're expecting to get. It's about what you're expected to give."
MODERN PROVERB

Defining idea . . .

Don't be afraid to expect good behavior and discuss with your partner tactics for discipline. Be prepared to compromise, but remember that whatever the rights of the children, it is your home, too. Never forget that every member of the family is entitled to respect even if the love takes longer to grow.

How did it go?

Q   I think my teenage stepson has a crush on me. How can I deal with this?

A   *This is a common problem when the stepmother is a lot younger than the father. Don't mention anything to your stepson for a month or so—teenage crushes are over as quickly as they start—then get your husband to discuss it with him. If you stay out of the situation it will be a lot less embarrassing for your stepson when he gets over it.*

Q   What should I do? My stepdaughter is fiercely loyal to her mother and sees me as a threat.

A   *Reassure her that you respect her love and loyalty for her mother and emphasize that you would like a completely different relationship with her. Never make negative comments about her mother and show interest and respect when your stepdaughter discusses her.*

33

Grandparents—the forgotten casualties

Grandparents are the overlooked casualties of divorce. In this idea we will look at the ways in which grandparents are affected by divorce and what they can do so they don't become a forgotten statistic.

Everyone focuses on the couple divorcing and, of course, the welfare of any child of a broken marriage is paramount. But who remembers the grandparents? What happens to the relationship between grandparents and grandchildren when divorce rocks their world?

THE SPECIAL RELATIONSHIP

Many couples are often stunned that their parents relate to their grandchildren in a way they never experienced during their own childhood. Parents who were notoriously stern and uncompromising act like human marshmallows when their

131

Here's an
idea for
you . . .

Do you see less of your grandchildren than you did before the divorce? If so, try these simple ideas to keep in contact. Do you miss reading to your grandchildren? Well, you don't have to. Record chapters of a book on tape and put them in the mail for a bedtime treat. Children love to get mail, so start sending cards, snapshots, letters, and silly drawings to them regularly. Get online and send emails and jokes, and what about a webcam to have some face-to-face contact? Text-messaging is a great way to stay in frequent contact cheaply, and instant messaging on your computer gives you the feel of a real conversation.

grandchildren arrive. It seems the love a grandparent has for a grandchild is truly unconditional. The perfect little children of their own offspring become the center of their world in an instant. The tragedy is that it only takes an instant for the center of their world to be knocked from their reach entirely.

So, why does this special relationship exist in the first place? There are many reasons why such a strong bond can be formed, not least because the love grandparents have for their grandchildren includes all the love they also have for their own child. It's a double whammy of feeling, but unfortunately one that's open to double the jeopardy when divorce looms.

Grandparents can have the best of both worlds—all the love for their grandchildren without all of the responsibility of their upbringing. They can be a shoulder to cry on and a trusted friend in a way a parent can't. There is a special relationship between the young and the old that no one can quite describe. Put simply, the grandparental relationship is magical.

REALITY CHECK

Divorce kills many things. And one fatality is magic. With so many things to consider during the process of divorce, it is perhaps unsurprising that some things are forgotten. However, it is not acceptable to forget about the feelings of the grandparents.

In some cases, grandparents are far from forgotten. When a couple with children divorces, one partner inevitably becomes a single parent. If that parent has to work full-time, childcare becomes an important issue. Rather than using an expensive, and often impersonal, day care service or nursery, many parents ask the grandparents to step into the breach.

Almost all take on this responsibility willingly and with love, but many also do so with a heavy heart. Grandparents who had planned and saved for their retirement can find themselves thrown into a very different life. Day-to-day care of their grandchildren can be a strain on financial resources as well as their energy reserves—young children can be tiring, older children emotionally draining.

Of course, the grandparents will be concerned about the effects that the divorce is having on their child as well as their grandchild. Divorce can cause emotional trauma similar to bereavement for all concerned. Grandparents often have few legal rights of access to their

Try another idea . . .

Suddenly a stepgrandparent and not sure how to deal with it? Take a look at IDEA 32, *The wicked stepparent*, for advice.

Defining idea . . .

"Divorce makes grandparents feel as though all that unconditional love they have to give is suddenly surplus to requirements."
TONY PARSONS, *Man and Boy*

grandchildren and can be left with no contact at all. They can also feel deeply saddened by the loss of a son- or daughter-in-law and understandably feel unable to express this grief to their own child.

Remarriage after divorce is another factor that can affect grandparents. It can take their own grandchildren even farther away from them physically and emotionally, and it can also present them with a set of stepgrandchildren.

Grandparents can find it hard to accept a replacement son- or daughter-in-law for a number of reasons—loyalty to the ex-spouse or protective feelings toward their own child being the most common. Equally, accepting their stepgrandchildren can bring its own problems, especially when those stepgrandchildren are teenagers. No bond has been created as they grow with cuddles, kisses, and games in the yard, and it can take much time and patience to create a workable relationship. However, grandparents, step or otherwise, can provide stability and support during the trauma of a divorce.

Then there are the cases when it is the grandparents themselves who divorce, leaving their families shocked and their grandchildren behind. It can be particularly difficult for grandfathers to keep in touch with their grandchildren in these situations as bonds are often created through the maternal line.

Whatever the situation, grandparents are special to a family, and as such should be central to it, too.

Q   **I've tried letters and emails but I still feel I'm losing touch with my grandchild's life. What else can I do?**

How did it go?

A   *How about exchanging scrapbooks? Make up a scrapbook of everything you're doing in your life. A picture of a cake you made, a bit of grass from the garden stuck in with glue, a squirt of your favorite perfume, a picture of you fixing the car, and a silly joke will work great.*

Q   **What legal rights do I have to see my grandchildren?**

A   *This varies greatly, so it's best to take legal advice. But you and your grandchild do have a moral right to a loving relationship with each other.*

34

Second time around

Or third . . . or fourth . . . It seems even the trauma of divorce can't keep us away from marriage. Make sure you see the reality, not just the romance. This will help you stop making the same mistakes again, and again . . .

Marriage can be addictive—I recently met a man who introduced me to his fifth wife! Many of us go through our divorce swearing we'll never marry again, only to find ourselves walking up the aisle a year or two later.

THE MARITAL MERRY-GO-ROUND

The grief and bitterness involved in divorce fade with time and leave many of us realizing that despite the risks, we're still made for sharing. However, we are still horribly prone to making the same mistakes over and over. When entering into a second marriage it's vital to have your head and your heart working together. Rushing into a new marriage on the rebound is the emotional equivalent of shooting yourself in the foot, and can leave you with a permanent limp.

Here's an idea for you . . .

Learn from your mistakes. Draw up a table and list the mistakes both you and your ex made in your first marriage. Ask yourself hard questions about your own contribution to the breakdown of your marriage, and try to see your ex's mistakes without a screen of bitterness. Having this in black and white will act as a reminder of potential pitfalls in new relationships and help you focus on any unresolved issues you need to conquer before committing to someone new.

That all sounds sensible, but you're in love and, surely, that's enough to make it work this time, isn't it? Although I may sound harsh, it's even less likely that love alone will be enough to make a second marriage work. Second marriages often have even more challenges, such as stepfamilies or unresolved emotional baggage from the first marriage.

That's not to say remarrying is a bad idea. If you go into a second marriage properly prepared and fully self-aware, then it has a great chance of staying the course. Think about it. This time you're getting married with more years of experience and maturity under your belt. You've experienced the realities of marriage and the desolation of divorce and are still committed to trying again.

However, it's important that you don't view your previous marriage as a failure. It's far healthier to see it as a valuable life experience. There's no going back and you can't change the fact that you shared a marriage with that person, so don't waste time regretting it. Instead learn from it, then put it aside and move on.

THE SECRET FORMULA

There is no secret formula for making marriage work because we are all so different. And far from that being a problem, I see it as a huge strength. No marriage is doomed because statistics say so, and no second marriage is destined to be problematic just because the first one was. It's simply up to us.

Any relationship has to have strong foundations to support it through its life, and this is especially true of a second marriage. Patience, understanding, commitment, and adaptability are the foundations that will support your love for each other and allow it to grow. Basing a new relationship on anything superficial such as charm, money, or sexual attraction will give you a far rockier ride in the future.

That's not to say that a good sexual relationship or financial stability is unimportant, but these elements should be approached with awareness and maturity. You'll need to abandon romantic fantasies and keep your hormones in check if you're looking for a long-term relationship. Of course, you can let them out to play once in a while, but make sure the foundations are in place too before you fly up the aisle.

Try to be aware of each other's needs and ask yourself if you can love your new partner in the way they need to be loved, not just in the way you want to. Discuss each other's emotional baggage from previous relationships so you

Worried about becoming a step-parent? Look at IDEA 32, *The wicked stepparent*, and see how best to "step" into your new shoes.

Try another idea . . .

"The art of love ... is largely the art of persistence!"
ALBERT ELLIS, psychologist and author

Defining idea . . .

have an awareness of each other's potential trigger points, but then put it firmly in lost baggage. Be aware of—and know you can accept—each other's flaws and feel comfortable with the fact that if they never change from how they are now, you will still love them.

Discuss your individual circumstances and work on ways of fitting them together. Sort out practicalities such as finance and commitments to previous marriages and existing children before you get married.

If you focus on honesty, trust, fidelity, and flexibility you'll be tying a strong knot of love between you that will stay securely fastened in the future.

Q **How can I be sure I'm not remarrying for the wrong reasons?**

How did it go?

A *Ask yourself some searching questions about what your reasons are. Are you marrying because you're lonely? Because it makes the finances easier? Because you need a parent for your children? Or is it because you truly love this person? Do you bring out the best in each other? Are you aware of each other's needs and feelings? Answer truthfully and take some time to fully analyze why you want to remarry.*

Q **Is it wise to seek counseling before I remarry?**

A *Do you feel there are unresolved issues you need to address before you commit to a new marriage? Do you feel you need outside help to do so? If the answer is yes, then seek some advice from a couples counselor. Some people find it useful to have a premarital counseling session either individually or with their partner even if there aren't specific issues to address. Discuss how you feel with your partner and move on from there.*

35

Save it or spend it?

So, separation seems inevitable and divorce is looming. It's time to begin thinking about money. This idea provides smart finance for the soon-to-be single.

Everyone's telling you horror stories about the money pit that was their divorce. Now you don't know if you should start stuffing your money under the mattress or just spend it while you've still got it.

FINANCIAL PLANNING

As well as placing a huge emotional strain on you, divorce can also strain your finances. Not only do you have to consider how best to divide your financial assets, but you also have to consider the cost of the divorce itself.

The best way to cope with the financial aspects of separation and divorce is to start planning for all the monetary ramifications as soon as possible. Many of us can see our divorce coming from a long way off and, although we may not want to face up to it sooner than we have to, it pays to plan.

Here's an idea for you . . .

If you know divorce is on the way, give your life a financial spring cleaning before the funds disappear:

- **Pay off any outstanding credit card bills**
- **Get your car serviced**
- **Go the dentist, optician, or have any treatment done while you still have benefits**
- **Buy yourself good work clothes for interviews or court appearances**
- **Stock the pantry and wine rack, and stock your favorite aftershave or bath soap**

The first thing to work out is exactly how much your lifestyle costs you. Look at bank statements, credit cards, and loan repayments to analyze your spending patterns. Then divide your spending into sections. Some examples include: house (mortgage and maintenance), car (repayments, gas, and upkeep), children (school/college fees, clothing, etc.), food, clothing, travel to work, socializing, and vacations. By establishing an overview of your spending, you'll be able to work out what your ongoing financial needs will be.

After you've analyzed your current finances, estimate how much the divorce is likely to cost you. Will it be fast and straightforward or long, drawn-out, and expensive? Will you incur attorneys' fees and court costs? If so, what are the hourly rates? Perhaps you'll need auxiliary divorce services, such as accountants, financial advisors, private investigators, or counselors.

Once you have a rough idea of the costs involved, check to see if you have enough liquid funds to cover them. If not, be aware that the costs may have to be met out of larger assets, such as equity in the matrimonial property.

PREEMPTIVE STRIKE

If you're getting divorced, the chances are it won't be that friendly. And although it may be hard to start to see your husband or wife as your adversary, it may be in your best interests to prepare for a financial fight.

Is your biggest financial asset your home? Check out IDEA 36, *Your place or mine?*, for tips on how to prevent your marital home from becoming a mine field.

Try another idea . . .

If all of your assets are in joint names, start thinking about establishing an individual financial identity. Open a bank account and apply for a credit card in your name. It's important to make sure you have a credit rating in case you wish to take out a loan or mortgage after your divorce.

Be aware of all non-liquid assets—in other words, the ones you can't spend now. So, calculate the value of any retirement savings, life insurance, or trusts. Also think about employee benefits—preferential rates on your mortgage, company car, or healthcare.

List everything you own, together or separately, and check for hidden assets. Get valuations done on your home and any valuable contents in it. Art, antiques, and collectibles are all viewed as part of your net worth.

Get recent bank, credit card, loan, and retirement savings statements and look at your own and your partner's paystubs. Be aware that bonus and commission payments may not be on the regular paystub. Also make sure that your name is on the deeds of your property and check for any joint liability on debts or loans.

"The real measure of wealth is how much you'd be worth if you'd lost all your money."
MODERN PROVERB

Defining idea . . .

Manage the financial process of your divorce at every stage. If necessary, contact an accountant to help you come to grips with your fiscal matters. If you're not earning at the moment and your spouse deals with the finances, get up to speed on household expenditures and all joint assets. The financial implications of divorce will kick in as soon as you separate, so get informed, not scared.

How did it go?

Q   How can I ensure my legal fees are reasonable?

A   *Negotiate with your spouse yourself as much as possible and then have your lawyer check any agreements. Don't allow your lawyer to write unnecessary letters you could do yourself. Contact the paralegal team for routine information and be aware of the costs for letters, emails, faxes, and phone calls. Pay fees on time to avoid interest charges and keep all contact with your lawyer brief and to the point. Don't be tempted to lengthen proceedings out of spite—this will eat up your share of the assets.*

36

Your place or mine?

Your house or apartment is probably the biggest asset you have and it may become the biggest bone of contention between you. Learn how to stop the marital home from morphing quickly into a battleground.

You don't really want to end up fighting over somewhere that was once your home, do you? But getting a perspective on property can be a hard thing to do, especially when so much money is involved. However, there are peacekeeping steps you can take.

HOLD FIRE ON THE HOME FRONT

Unless substantial investments have been made elsewhere, the home holds the most financial value and any equity will provide the bulk of a financial settlement. However, a question often posed during financial negotiations is whether the house should be sold at all. This can be a tricky one to answer and can slow down the entire proceedings of the divorce.

Here's an idea for you . . .

Resolve to become a sensible seller. This may sound obvious, but how much experience do you have selling something as valuable as your home? You need the best deal you can get to ensure your financial future, so follow this advice for the best results. Get at least three written market valuations from real estate agents who know your area and accompany the agent around the house pointing out particular features. Work out if you will accept offers or only the asking price and advertise online to ensure you reach potential buyers countrywide as well as locally.

For example, take a couple who have lived for fifteen years in a modest three-bedroom house in the suburbs. The mortgage has been greatly reduced over the years, the equity is substantial, and the wife wishes to continue living in the house with the couple's two children. However, there are no other financial investments of note to enable the husband to buy a home elsewhere and he may have to resort to renting.

This kind of situation is quite common and it can be difficult to find a solution. A couple will have worked hard over the years to pay off the mortgage, but with no other financial assets, how can a fair settlement be reached after divorce? Well, sometimes the house remains the property for the custodial parent, with financial balance being achieved by giving the other parent a lion's share of other assets. But this does have its down sides. A house is, in general, an appreciating asset. In other words, it grows in value over time. Investments will appreciate, too, depending on how the money has been invested and the state of the financial markets, but it is liable to tax. This should be considered when making a settlement.

Usually if there is substantial equity in a house, the best decision is to sell. This enables both parties to re-house using the money from the sale without adversely affecting either one.

Is your home just part of your financial nightmare? Read IDEA 35, *Save it or spend it?*, and end your bad dreams.

Try another idea . . .

The mortgage viability of both parties also needs to be considered. For example, if the custodial parent retains the house, will she also be able to afford the mortgage payments? If she is not working, a bank may refuse to let her take on the mortgage at all.

FOR SALE

So you've decided to sell the house and split the proceeds. At this point it is important to consider that your property is not just an asset, it's also your home and it may have been the center of your life for many years. It's bound to be full of memories, good and bad, and it may be a real wrench to let it go.

Focusing on your house as an asset, rather than a home, can help you get through the process, but remember too the feelings of any children involved. Moving away from a home, school, or area can be an upheaval of the worst kind for both parents and children, so get as much support from friends and family as possible.

"I am a marvelous housekeeper. Every time I leave a man I keep his house."
ZSA ZSA GABOR

Defining idea . . .

Your home may well have been your emotional security as well as your financial security and you might want to hold on to it no matter what. However, this can store up trouble for later. Ask yourself some hard questions when making the decision to sell or stay:

- Are the costs of the mortgage, maintenance, insurance, and taxes too much for me?
- Is it too big for me?
- Will it remind me of my past and prevent me from moving into my future?
- Will it drain my resources, energy, and time?

If you answer yes to any of these questions, selling, even though it's difficult, may be the best solution.

Q **My name isn't on the mortgage, but I've lived in the house with my husband for fifteen years. Do I have a share in it or not?**

How did it go?

A *Check to see if your name is on the deed to the property. If it is, you do jointly own it. If not, your ownership may be in question even though your marriage has been a reasonably long one. Contact an attorney to clarify your position ASAP because, without your name on the deed, your husband could sell without your consent.*

Q **I'm planning on giving my wife our house as a one-time settlement. How can I ensure she wills the house to our children rather than any new partner or children she has?**

A *You may be able to stipulate she wills the property or proceeds to your children as part of your financial agreement. Consult an attorney to check out your legal position and ensure any agreements between you and your wife are legally notarized.*

And now, time for something completely different

You feel like you've climbed the metaphorical Mount Everest, so why not try it for real? Doing something positive will get your post-divorce life off to a great start.

Many people decide to break out of the mold and redefine themselves when a divorce is over. After all, everything else in your life has changed, so maybe it's time to bite the bullet and do something different.

THE NEED FOR CHANGE

It's true that divorce changes lives forever. However, change should not be seen as negative. It's very easy to feel dragged down and depressed by the process of divorce, but a great way to get through the dark days is to focus on the opportunities that lie ahead. Of course, these opportunities may not be the ones you thought you'd have when you got married, but they will be exciting and vibrant nonetheless.

Here's an idea for you . . .

Seize your opportunity: Think of that something different you might do. The trick here is to base it on something that interests you. For example, if you like travel, simply put a different spin on it. Instead of lying on the beach in Morocco, trek the Atlas Mountains. If you're interested in the environment, take a sabbatical and get involved in an ecotourism trip. Interested in other cultures? Then learn Arabic or Swahili online. Open your mind and *expect* to achieve different things. This shift to positive thinking alone will enable you to do whatever you want.

Think about it. When you were married you had to consider your spouse. You had to take his views, likes, and dislikes into consideration. Perhaps your own needs and desires were subjugated because of this. Maybe you were the one forever compromising and putting what you wanted aside for the sake of the marriage. Those times are over! The divorce is through, you've allowed yourself some time to grieve, and now you're ready to implement some positive change and move on.

So, what is it you really want to do? You know you've got an opportunity to make some decisions entirely of your own, but do you not have a clue where to start? Don't panic! This is normal. Even the things you dreamed about as a way to get through the divorce often fade and seem intangible when the process is finally over. The mere fact that you *can* choose whatever you want to do can sometimes be paralyzing.

How do you get out of that paralysis and start to move things forward when you're scared of change? Well, try to accept your fear. Realize that change after divorce is inevitable, and that the fear of moving on alone is normal. Don't give yourself a hard time. Instead try to understand why you might feel this way.

Realize that you've been focused on a single outcome—that of finalizing your divorce. Once that focus has gone you may feel cut adrift and a little lost. To get back on track you simply have to focus on your goals and take things step by step.

Want to do something different, but you're concerned about finances? Take a look at IDEA 35, *Save it or spend it?*, for advice.

Try another idea . . .

ACTION PLAN

The first thing to do is write down your ambitions and start to work out practical ways to achieve them. Okay, but what if you don't have any? Even better! You can really allow your imagination to roam and create an action plan from scratch.

Many people feel the need to do something completely different when a marriage has ended. They want to experience something outside the norm and something that no one would have expected them to do when they were married. This is a way of expressing your regained individuality after divorce.

After my divorce I trained to walk the Great Wall of China for charity. Being small and a bit on the delicate side, no one really thought I could do it. This made me all the more determined. With the help of a sympathetic trainer at the gym, I got fit. I ran, I rowed, I did things with weights I only thought bodybuilders did, and pretty quickly I became fit, strong, and prepared for anything.

I also went out and raised money. I convinced people in my local community that if I could train for something as arduous as walking along an ancient wall in the Gobi Desert, then they could donate a bit of cash.

"Shoot for the moon; even if you miss you'll land among the stars."
LEE BROWN, writer

Defining idea . . .

155

The sense of achievement was immense. I regained my self-respect and I gained the respect of others. It gave me a great focus and stopped my dwelling on the sadness of my divorce. Best of all, it was something completely different. I'd proved to myself that I could be anyone I wanted to be if I put my mind to it. And I assure you, if I can do it, you can, too!

How did it go?

Q   Isn't doing something different just a temporary escape?

A   *Not if you view it the right way. That's why it's important to base your "different" thing in your reality—in other words an interest you already have. That way you'll be able to develop a latent part of your character and explore new areas of achievement. Divorce can be an experience that shrinks your confidence, and this exercise is a way to make it grow again.*

Q   You joke about climbing Everest, but now that I'm divorced I'd love a physical challenge like that. How do I go about it?

A   *There are all sorts of physical challenges you can take part in, often for charity, and a quick web search will get you started. Climbing Mount Kilimanjaro is a great start as it's more of a walk than a climb. Expeditions to Everest can cost around $2,000 and take about seven weeks. Be prepared for altitude sickness, frostbite, and sunburn, but there are benefits—you need to eat 6,000 calories a day!*

38

Moving on

Whether you're itching to buy a place of your own now or you're planning to rent until the dust settles, this idea takes a look at the pros and cons of renting or buying property after a divorce.

The divorce decree has landed in the mailbox and you're now free to move on with your life. But have you decided where you'll be moving on to? You know you want to move on emotionally, but do you want to move geographically, too?

HOME SWEET HOME

Divorce throws your world upside down. It forces you to make big decisions and sometimes the responsibility of trying to make the right ones can be terrifying.

Many of us find our marital properties sold to provide the financial settlement for

Here's an idea for you . . .

Choose two similar properties in the same area—one to buy and one to rent. Then work out what your monthly payments would be on a mortgage for the first property and multiply by twelve. Then add any taxes you'd need to pay. For the rental property multiply the monthly rent by twelve and add any taxes or fees. For both, add any furniture or fittings you'd need to buy. Compare the results. Buying can be an investment in the long term but very expensive now, while with renting the opposite applies. Do the math and see what suits your circumstances now and in the long term.

both parties. This, of course, leaves us with the pressing issue of where to live. Grown adults can even end up living back with their elderly parents because they have no other options. Others rent for a while before buying, and some people buy right away. But the question remains, what is the right solution for you?

The first thing to be aware of is your own emotional state. Are you ready to make a decision now or do you need some time to get your head together? If you do feel emotionally rocky, then renting for a while could be a good solution. Although you'll get no financial return on the cash investment you make in terms of paying rent, there are other benefits.

Renting means that the ultimate responsibility for the property is not yours. Of course, you have to care for it and treat it with respect, but if the roof falls down or the stove quits, then it's not your financial problem. That can be a liberating thought after the weighty responsibilities of divorce.

If you rent, you also have the freedom to move on after your lease expires so you needn't make any long-term commitment to either a property or an area. You don't have to take out a mortgage and you can keep your assets liquid and flexible. On the other hand, there is no real stability in renting. If you buy a property, you're usually making a wise financial investment, market conditions permitting. Buying is often a good decision to make after a divorce, especially if your settlement has taken the form of a lump sum and you have no pensions or other investments to secure your future. Buying a property can also help you feel stable and rooted.

Do you want to stay put in the marital home, but it's proving a struggle? IDEA 36, *Your place or mine?*, explores the issue.

Try another idea . . .

It's not an easy decision to make, but come on, you're used to that now!

FACTS AND FIGURES

The question of whether it's financially more prudent to buy or rent property is hotly debated. Many people assume that owning a property is always a better deal and renting is "throwing your money down the drain." Others feel that in a volatile financial climate renting is by far the best option.

There are general principles that you can follow to lead you through this argument, but they are by their nature general and not always correct for every circumstance. If you're living in a society where the property market has peaked and the financial indicators suggest the country may go into decline or even a recession, then it is better to rent. This way you have a chance to sit tight until property values fall and stabilize before buying. Buying on the crest of a wave is never a good idea.

"Home is any four walls that enclose the right people."
HELEN ROWLAND, journalist

Defining idea . . .

159

If you are planning to live in a large metropolitan area where prices are always high, renting can be the better option. This is unless you can get a good deal on a property, or you're planning to live there for a long time, in which case your property will usually appreciate in value. If you live in an area where property prices are reasonable and there have been no peaks or troughs in the market for some time, it is probably best to buy. However, these principles are general and don't always serve to provide the best solution for an individual, especially when divorce is involved.

How did it go?

Q   How can I get a good landlord?

A   *Go through a rental agency rather than renting privately. Sign a lease agreement to make sure your rights are protected as well as the landlord's. With the agent, make an inventory of everything in the property and its condition and both sign it. This should avoid any disputes later.*

Q   Do I have to be employed to get a mortgage?

A   *In general, yes. You need to be able to prove a steady income for at least six months. However, in the case of women returning to work after divorce, lenders can be more flexible. They will also take into account any regular income you have from nonworking sources, such as trusts.*

39

Kick-start your career

Maybe you've been out of the workforce for years. Or maybe you've just been bringing in the bacon. Well, now you've got the opportunity to create an exciting new future for yourself.

Why not reevaluate your career? Divorce has meant that you've gotten out of a domestic and emotional rut and now's your chance to do the same with your job. So, go on, kick-start your career.

IT'S NEVER TOO LATE

Many people feel that once they hit forty, some invisible threshold has been reached and it's now too late to do anything new. After all, by that time academic or professional training has usually been completed, retirement plans established, and mortgages undertaken. To do something new becomes risky and many of us stick with the same job we've always had because it's comfortable and safe.

Here's an idea for you . . .

Discover what you really want to do. Write down ten things that you love doing. This can include absolutely anything. Then narrow that list to the three things that are most important and think of any jobs that include them. If you get stuck, do an Internet search on those choices to give you some ideas, or brainstorm the problem with friends. Think laterally and you'll soon come up with a number of different jobs. Now you can begin applying or training and get started on the ladder to that dream career.

But what happens when divorce turns our lives upside down? Nothing seems safe anymore, and whether we're thirty-five or fifty-five we may find ourselves forced to make career choices that are neither easy nor comfortable. Because we can never guarantee what life will throw our way, there is little point in thinking that we are ever too old to change our lives.

Change can be scary, but it can be exciting, too. Suddenly you're faced with returning to work and you're not sure where to start. Perhaps you're a divorced woman and you haven't been in the workforce for twenty years. You're going to be scared; that's normal. So, just accept that you will feel nervous about your new situation and stop giving yourself such a hard time.

Instead of panicking and hurling yourself at the first job available, take some time to evaluate your options and find a job that suits you. Remember that everyone is entitled to a job that is challenging, interesting, and rewarding. This is especially true if you've just coped with the emotional and financial stresses involved with divorce.

CHANGING DIRECTION

Whether you're returning to work after a long gap or just taking the opportunity to change your career path, there are many ways to ensure you end up doing something you really want to do. You might not fall into your dream job overnight, but you can ensure that every step you take is one toward it.

That all sounds great, but how do you go about it? First of all start to think about this process positively. Even if you're being forced back into work or to change your job through financial necessity, see it as a challenge and an opportunity.

Fed up with everyone telling you what you should be doing? Have a look at IDEA 22, *Don't do it like that—do it like this!*, for help with unwanted advice.

Try another idea . . .

Immediately start to network. Tell everyone you know that you are looking for a new job. Give a copy of your updated resume to people you think might be able to help and ask them to pass it on, too. You'll be surprised how quickly this can yield results.

Update your skills. Ask former colleagues or agencies what skills and qualifications are now relevant to your industry and sign up for any necessary courses. Even if you're still in the process of updating your skills as you apply for jobs, it will show employers you are committed to making a success of your career.

Look at all the options for retraining. Many colleges offer financial help and have counseling and day-care facilities at reduced cost. Going back to college isn't always financially viable so look at distance learning and online courses. Also look at options where you can earn and train at the same time. Careers in teaching and health care often offer generous grants while you train. Many colleges offer part-time and evening courses, allowing you to continue to work while you study.

"The roots of true achievement lie in the will to become the best you can become."
HAROLD TAYLOR, philosophical thinker

Defining idea . . .

If you're already working and would like to change direction, see what options are available within your existing company. Many larger companies can offer training and job swaps, or may even be able to send you on an outside course.

Broaden your approach to getting a job in the area you want. If you'd like to be a doctor but can't afford the time or cost of training, don't dismiss that area entirely. Instead look at other options within health care—nursing, management, counseling, and lab work could all be options you could consider.

How did it go?

Q   There are a number of avenues I could take, but how do I choose which is the right one?

A   Why not try temping or freelancing for a while in each one? There are many specialist employment agencies that provide temporary work allowing you to try out all sorts of industries before you commit full-time to one in particular.

Q   I haven't worked for years and I feel overwhelmed. How do I even get started?

A   Be logical and methodical in your approach and look at the skills you already have. You will find that running a home or raising children will give you skills in management, finance, and counseling without even knowing you have them. Isolate these skills and then apply them to a job.

40

Staying friends

Can you stay friends with your ex? Do you even want to? After the weapons of divorce have been put down, you can take things a stage further and make a lasting peace. And it can be worth it.

Staying friends with an ex-spouse can be an uphill struggle, but it can also be an achievable and worthwhile goal, especially if you have children. Here we'll look at the pros and cons of staying friends and achieving intimacy without sex with your ex.

FRIENDLY OR FRIENDS?

Is it really possible to create a real friendship with the man or the woman you've just divorced? Well, a lot depends on how and why you split up, whether you had a smooth or acrimonious divorce, and how you both feel now. If your divorce was bitter, it's unlikely you'll be meeting each other for a cappuccino to catch up anytime soon. If, however, the decision to get divorced was a mutual one, the process went

Here's an idea for you . . .

Respect is essential for a successful friendship. No matter what has gone before in your relationship, you must learn to respect each other as friends even if you couldn't as husband and wife. A good way of doing this is to instigate "divorce vows." A useful alternative to marriage vows, these can keep you on the straight and narrow. Work together to draw up an acceptable agreement. Examples could include not asking your children to keep secrets from your ex and not rehashing the old conflicts of your marriage.

smoothly, and the broken dishes were kept to a minimum, then you've got a much better chance of staying friends.

You also need to ask yourself why you want to stay friends when staying married was an impossibility. If you didn't want to get divorced and you'll do anything to keep your ex in your life, this is a really bad reason to pursue a friendship because the motives for doing so are based on trying to regain the intimacy of the past relationship rather than seeking to create something new. If the marriage has failed, the special bond of husband and wife cannot be re-created through platonic friendship and the relationship you do create will always be a disappointment.

Many couples want to stay friends because of their children. If you have children you could be saving them and yourself a lot of grief if you can achieve a friendship with the other parent. Animosity between parents is always destructive to the children involved and can also be destructive to the relationship they have with you. Successful coparenting demands cooperation and this can't be achieved if you communicate with each other through shouting and screaming. The purity of the motive to make things better for the kids can often help you get past the hurt and the bitterness of your divorce and into a positive and productive relationship.

ABSOLUTE FRIENDSHIP

If you have decided to be friends with each other after the divorce is final then it can be achieved even if it's a difficult process. My own parents get on far better now as friends than they ever did in twenty-six years of marriage, and that's the case with many divorced couples of all ages.

Even if your divorce has been amicable, the divorce process trains you to view each other as adversaries, and you will need some time to let these feelings of conflict pass before you can move on as friends. Coping with divorce is an emotional process and it's important to recognize the stages that you may go through.

You may experience stages of anger, grieving, and healing in much the same way you would if you were bereaved. Understanding what stage you're at will help you in your goal to become friends with your ex.

Go at the speed of the person who has been most hurt by the process. If you've asked for a divorce and already moved in with your new partner, then your ex may need some considerable time to get over it before she asks you over for drinks. If you're still angry with your spouse, then acknowledge your feelings, but don't act on them. You may still have to communicate with your ex and you're not going to achieve a friendly relationship if you're still screaming at him on the phone.

Maybe you don't want to keep your ex in your life, so take a look at IDEA 13, *Cutting ties*, and move on.

Try another idea . . .

"The only way to have a friend is to be one."
RALPH WALDO EMERSON

Defining idea . . .

Stop looking to your ex for answers and resolutions. Your marriage has ended and it's time to move forward. Friendship will be much easier to establish if you're able to achieve closure on any residual negative emotions, and giving up blame is an important step in this. Accepting mutual responsibility is a far healthier way of moving forward.

Slowly work up to a level of friendship you're both comfortable with. There's no doubt that the first year after divorce will be the hardest, so start by simply being polite and courteous in your communications.

How did it go?

Q   My hateful ex has taken me for every penny I've got. Can I really be friends with her?

A   *Probably not! Contrary to popular belief there is a thick line between love and hate and in your case, keeping your ex in your life will cause more heartache. It's time to cut ties and move on.*

Q   Is it acceptable to be friends with my ex's new partner?

A   *If you're all comfortable with the situation then yes. After all, you both married the same spouse so you've got something in common. It can often help if there are children involved, but keep your ex's feelings in your thoughts, too. Sharing confidences about them is always a mistake. Keep the friendship on neutral ground and it may well work.*

41

Courtly love

Understanding the law can be confusing at the best of times, and if you have to appear in court it can be downright scary. If you're not prepared you might get more muddled than a mouse in a maze.

If your view of an attorney is a slightly sketchy-looking guy in a suit, then maybe it's time to demystify the court and get inside your attorney's briefs.

ORDER IN THE COURT

Going to court for the first time can be a bewildering experience. Your emotions will be highly strung from the general stress of the divorce and now you have to appear in front of a judge. Many people say that appearing in court makes them feel like they've done something wrong. With divorce, this is definitely not the case. Your hearing is "civil" and not "criminal"—no one is being criminally charged or will be prosecuted. However, the full force of the legal system can be overwhelming if you're unprepared. This idea aims to take the fear out of appearing in court and to help you be calm, confident, and in control when you're there.

Here's an idea for you . . .

Get rid of some of your nerves: visit the court in advance. If you've never been to court before, a practice run can be an excellent way to demystify the proceedings. Talk to your legal team and arrange to have a tour around the court. Visit the room your case will be heard in and become familiar with the layout of the court. That way you can visualize the hearing and be prepared for unexpected things like security searches and metal detectors. A visit will allow you to work out how much time it takes to get there, what the atmosphere is like, and will help the court feel more familiar and less frightening.

So, why do you have to go to court anyway? Well, in general you'll be asked to appear in court if you and your spouse can't reach a mutually acceptable financial agreement or the divorce itself is being contested by one party. Court hearings may involve ongoing maintenance disputes as well as determining a final settlement when the divorce is completed. You'll work with your attorney in preparing your case first and then your attorney will present this in court.

But what happens if you feel intimidated by the whole idea of having a court date? It is a common reaction. We're used to seeing scary trials depicted on television, but in reality, they're rarely as glamorous or as intimidating. These hearings are generally held in private and only the parties concerned, their legal representatives, and witnesses can enter the courtroom.

COPING WITH COURT

Since the formality of the occasion can make the experience very intimidating, it's important to constantly remind yourself that you haven't done anything wrong and that the aim of the hearings is simply to ensure that a fair settlement is reached. No one is there to punish you, even if it sometimes feels that everything is going against you.

It's also important to feel comfortable with your legal team. There's no point employing people that make you feel overwhelmed or small. They should be there to help you, and it's vital to feel that you are getting the best out of them. Make sure you and your attorney are on the same page before you go to court, and if you don't feel comfortable, then remember it is your right to choose someone else to represent you. Write down any questions you have and take along any additional information you think might be useful. If you do feel intimidated by your legal representatives, just remember that you are their employer and without you, they would have no work.

To prepare for your day in court there are lots of things you can do that will demystify the proceedings and make you feel more relaxed. Ask any friends or family who have been through the same thing to describe the process to you, or look online or at the library for information about the way a court hearing works.

On the day of your hearing take someone along with you for support and ensure you have all the little things sorted out before you go. Take

Maybe you're having enough trouble with your attorneys even before the court gets involved. Have a look at IDEA 43, *Attorneys–saints or sinners?*, for advice that won't cost you a ton.

Try another idea . . .

"Common sense often makes good law."
WILLIAM O. DOUGLAS, judge

Defining idea . . .

171

along enough money for parking, train fare, or refreshments and take something to read in case you are kept waiting. Plan your route to court and leave enough time to cope with any delays.

Plan what you are going to wear. Smart dress is the best option as this will show the court that you are treating the hearing with respect and the appropriate level of seriousness. Doing these little things in advance will make you feel more comfortable on the day.

How did it go?

Q   Will I have to give evidence?

A   *Probably not at the first hearing. Usually your legal team will talk for you. If the proceedings continue to further hearings you may be cross-examined by the opposing attorneys, but your own legal team will prepare you in advance for this.*

Q   Is the court's decision on financial matters final?

A   *Yes. That's why you take your case to court—to achieve a definitive agreement. In some cases you may be able to appeal, but the decision made at the final hearing is generally binding.*

42

Spas, bars, and chocolate

Divorce can be an extremely stressful time. The trick is to be aware of exactly how stressed you are, what your needs are, and how you can meet them. Here's how to recognize when your stress levels are on the rise and how to relax in the right way.

We all know how easy it is to fall into bad habits when the stress levels rise to full volume. We're down in the dumps and before we know it, we're gobbling yet another chocolate bar or uncorking another bottle of wine. With everything else going on, you must make sure you're following a pattern of healthy living.

ADDICTIVE BEHAVIOR

So, what happens when our divorce has made us depressed, stressed, and totally fed up? Well, the aim here is to prevent you from turning into a human-shaped

Here's an idea for you . . .

We all need a boost sometimes, so devise a list of alternative treats you can quickly put into play when you're tempted to binge on bad things. Write the list down and pin it to relevant places around the house. The fridge, the wine rack, and the telephone are good starting points. Make sure you have different kinds of treats at different levels so there will always be one to suit your mood. Massage, a game of football with friends, a pedicure, a meal out with friends, a weepy movie, and a candlelit bath are all suggestions to get you started.

chocolate or from replacing your blood with red wine. But comfort eating is common worldwide. When we get depressed we reach for warming plates of starchy food, cans of soda, and endless sweets. The sugar rush instantly improves our mood, but soon afterward we're feeling worse than we did before. Why is that?

Sugary foods, or carbohydrates that quickly turn to sugar in the body, provide an instant energy lift, and chocolate gives us an endorphin rush as well. But these effects are temporary and we're soon feeling sluggish, bloated, or even hungry again.

There are two main problems with reaching for comfort foods in times of stress. One is health-related—they are foods devoid of proper nourishment, which give us little in the way of sustainable energy, and they are calorific and the cause of weight gain. The second problem is emotional—the low following a sugar high can plunge us further into depression and if we start to gain weight our self-esteem will also take a dive.

Sugar, just like alcohol, is addictive. Patterns of addictive behavior are formed quickly in times of stress and can be harder to break when we're feeling low. But you can avoid or break these patterns and learn to live a healthier lifestyle.

BREAKING THE PATTERN

Many people use alcohol instead of sugar as a source of comfort. Not only does it give us an instant high like sugar, but it also anesthetizes the pain we're feeling. Of course, it's natural to want some comfort when we're going through a painful divorce. We feel dreadful, everything seems to be going wrong, and all we're really asking for is a temporary release.

That's fine—in moderation. And that is the key here. Everyone is entitled to the occasional chocolate binge or wild night out at the bar when things get bad, but do not make it a regular event. When you realize that you haven't had a day without chocolate or a night without alcohol for months, then it's probably time to regain some balance in your life.

You know *why* you're doing this—for comfort and because you feel miserable. So, see this knowledge as positive. You've identified that you're stressed and that you do need something to help you through it.

But remember, there are plenty of healthy alternatives to make you feel better. First of all, talk to your family and friends; let them know that you're finding the divorce difficult and you need some support. If you want to go out and socialize, then think of ways you can without being tempted to drink too much.

Need a bit more help to make you feel better during this horrible time? IDEA 17, *Healing hands*, provides you with some answers.

Try another idea . . .

"Relaxation should at times be given to the mind the better to fit it for toil when resumed."
PERIANDER OF CORINTH

Defining idea . . .

175

The easiest way is to be the designated driver, but if that sounds duller than a night in with the Weather Channel, be a bit more creative. Go to the movies, go bowling, or join an exercise class. Dancing drunk is almost impossible, so unless the Electric Slice really is your thing try salsa lessons, jazz, or hip hop and take your mind off divorce.

And if you really want to relax and unwind without getting the sugar shakes, why not book yourself in for a spa treatment? You can go for an hour or a week. Have a massage or a manicure. And men enjoy the experience just as much as women.

Q **How can I justify visiting a spa when the divorce is costing a fortune?**

How did it go?

A *Everyone is entitled to a treat, and getting your stress levels down is essential. If money is a problem, look to local colleges that often offer treatments at reduced cost if done by a student. Buy yourself some bath oils you can use again and again, or get a friend to give you a relaxing hand massage.*

Q **Isn't trying to give up chocolate during a stressful divorce going to make me feel worse?**

A *No one's saying you should give it up. Just don't binge on it! A balanced diet that includes a bit of chocolate now and again will do you absolutely no harm. However, if you're relying on it as a regular form of comfort, simply substitute another type of treat occasionally.*

43

Attorneys—saints or sinners?

Love them or hate them, attorneys are vital unless your divorce is wholly straightforward. The trick here is finding a lawyer you feel confident in and one who isn't going to charge you your weight in gold.

With more than half of marriages ending in divorce each year in the United States alone, and more than a million worldwide, legal business is certainly booming. Don't let the lawyers, legalese, and litigation get you down. Do your research and prevent your attorney from sinning against you.

UNDER INSTRUCTION

No, this heading doesn't mean you should get a "learner attorney." Instead, it's there to remind you that your attorney is your employee. He is taking "instructions" from you and you pay him for his work. Therefore, there is no reason to feel intimidated

Here's an idea for you . . .

Use this checklist at an initial appointment to see if your attorneys are up to scratch. At the first meeting they should:
- **Outline different ways to resolve your problem including mediation or negotiation as well as litigation**
- **Discuss a schedule of costs with you, outlining their fees and any extras**
- **Outline an estimated timescale for the completion of your divorce, depending on its complexity**

by your lawyer. If you do, then find another one.

Your attorney is paid to settle your divorce and any related disputes as efficiently as possible. Naturally, they have a bias toward you as their client and they will try to secure the best outcome in your favor. But they should do so in a constructive and professional manner, avoiding protracted arguments, which will only end up costing you more money.

Divorce can have a major emotional and financial impact on all family members involved. If you can't settle matters fairly between you and your spouse, then it is inevitable that an attorney will become involved. You shouldn't feel frightened about this, or feel that things will work out badly because of it.

Many people, women in particular, feel that if they don't accept the initial offer that their spouse is making for a financial settlement and take on an attorney to check out their case, they will come out worse because of it. There is no reason why this should happen.

It is sensible to check out any offers being made with an attorney before accepting them, no matter how generous they seem to be. And it's easy to arrange an initial appointment with an attorney to check out your options. Law firms usually make these available at no charge or for a nominal fee.

Things are getting sticky and now you have to go to court. Don't panic—instead, check out IDEA 41, *Courtly love*, and prepare for a trip to court.

Try another idea . . .

An initial consultation will allow you to discuss your problem with a trained professional and then make an educated decision regarding whether or not you need legal representation. If you do decide to retain an attorney, then you can be assured that everything you discuss is confidential. You can also choose how your attorney contacts you. It's perfectly acceptable to have your correspondence sent to an alternate address or to receive calls on your cell.

TIME TO SOLICIT SOME ADVICE

There's no doubt about it, attorneys are expensive. Therefore, you want to make sure you choose one who is worth the fee. Despite the cost, there is no substitute for professional legal advice when things get sticky. A good attorney can save you a lot of money in the long run, especially if your case is complex. If you really can't afford legal representation then check out whether you're eligible for any legal aid or financial support.

"Lawyers are like rhinoceroses: thick-skinned, short sighted, and always ready to charge."
DAVID MELLOR

Defining idea . . .

181

So, how can you choose a good lawyer? Well, first of all you should make sure that your lawyer is a member of an accredited body and associated with a reputable firm. Personal recommendations and client testimonials are also a good starting point.

When you meet your attorney it's important that you feel you can develop a good working relationship, one in which you feel confident in your representation. An attorney is someone who should provide you with reliable advice regarding your case at all times and will explain anything you don't understand.

Good lawyers will acknowledge that whatever decisions need to be made are yours to make. They can guide and advise you legally, but they shouldn't push you into any decisions you feel uncomfortable with. They should also help you to understand the short- and long-term consequences of any decisions you do make. Whenever you see your attorney, take along any information you think might be relevant and always note down any questions you have before you go. Ask your attorney to confirm anything in writing that you want to be reminded of and make notes during the appointment if it's useful.

Your attorney should be capable and sympathetic, keen to resolve your disputes, and not just a necessary evil with outrageous fees.

Q   How can I keep my costs down and what hidden extras should I expect?

A   Using mediation services before going to an attorney can dramatically reduce your fees. Extras include filing fees, letters, phone calls, faxes, photocopying, and research, all of which may be charged on top of the hourly rate. Pay bills promptly to avoid interest charges.

Q   Can I change my attorney during the divorce proceedings if I'm unhappy?

A   Always check the contract you have with an attorney thoroughly before signing it. This will be sent to you at the beginning of your relationship with your lawyer. It will outline any notice period or penalties involved in terminating your instructions to them. But, yes, you are entitled to choose whoever you wish to represent you.

How did
it go?

44

Other cultures

Marriage has a religious basis so there are different rules governing divorce around the world. This idea provides a brief guide to how other cultures cope when it all goes wrong.

In July 2003, a Malaysian man successfully ended his marriage by text message. And everyone's heard of a quickie divorce in Las Vegas. But is it true that a Jewish man can divorce his wife by saying "I divorce you" three times? And are Muslim women allowed to divorce their husbands?

JEWISH DIVORCE

The Jewish religion has always recognized the concept of a no-fault divorce. For thousands of years it has felt that if a man and woman are unhappy in their marriage, then they should be able to break free from it. In fact the Talmud states

Here's an idea for you . . .

Do some research online about divorce in different cultures. See if you can apply any of their rules to your own case. This can be an interesting and fun way of making you feel better if your divorce is getting you down. For example, if you're feeling glum about having to make your maintenance payments then check out some of the astronomical sums paid out under Californian divorce law by browsing through a few divorce websites!

that a man is free to divorce his wife if she ruins his dinner or simply if he finds another woman more attractive. It even states that a man *must* divorce his wife if she has been sexually unfaithful to him—even if he doesn't want to! The Torah states that all the dissatisfied husband has to do is write a bill of divorce, hand it to his wife, and then send her away.

Given this, you could be forgiven for thinking that getting a divorce in Jewish law is easy-peasy. However, the Jewish rabbis quickly cottoned on to this and devised a set of procedures that made obtaining a divorce far from easy. They were keen to avoid men recklessly divorcing their wives and acting with little or no responsibility. So, there are now a huge array of rules regarding the writing, delivery, and acceptance of this bill, known as a "get."

Despite the relative ease with which a husband can divorce his wife, Jewish law does not allow a wife to initiate divorce proceedings herself. The Talmud also says that if a man wishes to divorce his wife, then she can't prevent him from doing so.

Some of these laws have eased a little over the past thousand years or so, and although a woman technically still cannot divorce her husband, a rabbinical court can compel him to

Look at IDEA 1, *Once upon a time . . .* , and check out the status of divorce worldwide.

Try another idea . . .

divorce her. This would happen if a woman could prove that her husband had violated his marital obligations, such as by failing to provide food, clothing, or sexual intercourse. The divorce could also be compelled if he was physically repugnant in some way and in certain cases because of sexual inadequacy!

DIVORCE AND ISLAM

Followers of Islam feel that marriage is prescribed by God and lawfully unites a man and woman in a relationship of mutual consent. They feel marriage should create a union of tranquillity and compassion, but, as in all cultures, that doesn't always happen.

Although Islam actively discourages divorce, it does recognize it is a reality and allows both a man and a woman to initiate divorce proceedings. There are guidelines for divorce both in the religious scriptures and in Islamic law, but the interpretation of them can sometimes be confusing. However, Muslims are encouraged at all times to exercise justice and kindness when bringing their marriage to a conclusion.

"Divorce unites the world in sorrow."
MODERN SAYING

Defining idea . . .

187

The Koran establishes the point that men and women have the right to divorce. But there are still few references to divorce within the Islamic holy book, and it's unclear as to the procedural roles that men and women take. When a divorce is initiated by the husband, it is known as the "talaq." The initiation may be verbal or written so long as the wife is in receipt of it. If a man is divorcing his wife in a no-fault situation, then he is required to repay the full dowry that she brought into the marriage. After the talaq there is a three-month waiting period during which the couple live under the same roof but they mustn't have sex with each other. This gives a cooling off period and time to see if the woman is pregnant. If she is, the waiting period increases until she has the child.

A divorce initiated by the woman is called a "Khu." If her husband is not at fault, then she has to pay him the sum of her dowry again as she is breaking the marriage contract. If she is divorcing him because he has broken the marriage contract, then she has to prove this to a judge. The judge will make his decision according to this proof and the wife has to abide by this.

Many Muslim women feel that men have absolute power in the realm of divorce, especially as the judges are always men themselves. There is great debate over this issue since, although the Koran states that there should be a "degree of difference" between the power structure in divorce, it is no more specific than that.

Q   **Can a religious court dissolve a marriage without civil proceedings in the United States?**

How did it go?

A   *No. All marriages have to be dissolved by civil law. However, the strict followers of the Jewish religion would not consider a couple to be divorced by civil proceedings alone. Their own procedures must be followed or any future marriages would be seen as bigamous and the children of them illegitimate.*

Q   **Does the Catholic Church recognize civil divorce?**

A   *According to its religious laws, divorce is not allowed. However, in practical terms the Church does recognize divorce, but it will not allow divorcees to remarry in a Catholic church.*

45

Honey, I need some money

Maintenance is a financial and emotional minefield, but if you both focus on your true needs, you're willing to compromise, and you put past misdemeanors aside, then amicable solutions can be reached.

If we're doling out money to our ex-spouse we invariably feel it's too much and if we're on the receiving end then we feel it's too little. So whether you call it alimony or maintenance, you'll soon discover that when it comes to money we all speak the same language.

FINDING THE FINANCE

Once your marriage has broken down and you've decided to separate, one of the first things you'll think about are the financial arrangements. How are you going to support yourself? How will the children be supported? Maybe you're the breadwinner and need to work out how much you can afford to pay your spouse in

Here's an idea for you . . .

When working out what your needs are in order to fix a maintenance amount, use this checklist to help you make a start.

- **Your income now and potentially**
- **Your spouse's income now and potentially**
- **Access to pensions and investments**
- **Housing arrangements for both of you**
- **The need to own a car**
- **Your budget for clothing, food, and entertainment**
- **Your legal fees during the divorce**
- **Maintenance needs for your children**

maintenance. Perhaps you're concerned about how you'll be able to afford to run two households now that you've split up.

This is where maintenance payments come in. The partner who is earning the greater amount of money will usually be required to make a payment to maintain the upkeep of his children and partner. This payment will be dependent on many things, but the defining point is the needs of both spouses and the needs of any children involved. There is often an interim period during which a figure for maintenance is set until the divorce has become final and the financial settlement has been agreed.

In the case of children under the age of eighteen, maintenance payments will be required to finance their food, shelter, clothing, and any fees or costs related to their education. Traditionally, children have lived with the mother, quite often in the former matrimonial home, and it is the father who paid the maintenance. However, this is changing. If the mother is the major breadwinner then she can either be the one paying maintenance, or simply not be entitled to any from her husband.

THE EMOTIONAL COST

Maintenance is always a thorny issue when couples split up and it can be an uphill struggle to come to an agreement that you both feel is fair. One of the main problems when discussing maintenance is that even though the issues are financial, they will be affected by your emotional perspective.

Many people, especially those affected by adultery or unreasonable behavior during their marriage, often feel a strong desire to penalize their partners financially. The final judgment on a settlement can take months to come to simply because one partner is set on financial revenge.

It is very hard to leave emotions behind when negotiating maintenance payments or financial settlements and few people manage it. However, it is rare that either spouse's past behavior during the marriage will actually affect the amount awarded by the court. The only time that the couple's actual behavior is taken into consideration is when current cohabitation occurs. In other words, if at the time of your separation one of you moves in with a new partner, or if this happens at any stage during the court proceedings, then this will have an impact on the maintenance agreement.

If you're going to court to settle your maintenance claim, have a look at IDEA 41, *Courtly love*, before you go.

Try another idea . . .

"If you think you have trouble supporting a wife, try not supporting her!"
ANONYMOUS

Defining idea . . .

193

A court will view cohabitation as relevant to the ongoing maintenance needs of the couple concerned for two reasons. First, if the claimant of maintenance is living with another person it will generally be assumed that they are receiving some form of financial support from that new partner. Second, if the payer of maintenance is cohabiting, it may be assumed that they are sharing their costs and therefore may have extra funds to contribute to the other spouse.

When fixing a maintenance order a court will try to keep parity between the couple concerned. So, if one partner has a large wage and the other is a homemaker, the homemaker will generally receive a large maintenance payment. However, the potential earning capacity of the homemaker will also be taken into consideration, as will whether they are still raising children at the time of the divorce.

Q   What does "financial parity" mean in real terms?

How did it go?

A   *Financial parity means that you both have a similar financial status. Think of it as maintaining a similar standard of living. So, if one of you is living in the former matrimonial five-bedroom house and the other in a rented one-bedroom apartment, a court may decide that the house should be sold. This is so that both parties can relocate to something similar and maintain a similar standard of living.*

Q   Will my maintenance payments stop if I remarry?

A   *In the case of a "clean break" where maintenance has been included in the lump sum of the settlement, the financial arrangements will not usually be affected. If the payments are made monthly then they may be affected. Seek advice from an attorney to find out what your position is.*

46

A passion for fashion

Maybe you're the best-dressed divorcees since Elizabeth Taylor and Richard Burton. If, on the other hand, your ties are still knitted and your shirts are shabby, now's the time for a makeover.

Once your divorce is through and you're feeling ready to move on, many people yearn for a bit of a change. If you don't feel like doing anything radical but do feel like trying something different, why don't you take a look at your wardrobe?

DRESS TO IMPRESS

Divorce can leave us with low self-esteem and very little in the way of confidence. We often feel rejected and unattractive and even though we may want to get out and socialize again, it can seem an intimidating prospect. This is a normal reaction and only to be expected after the trauma of divorce. But there are some easy ways

Here's an idea for you . . .

It can be difficult to know what really suits you, especially if you're shopping alone. So, try out a personal shopper. Don't panic, this isn't just a service for the rich. Of course you can go to an up-market store, but affordable stores are also offering personal shopping. Simply make an appointment, set a budget, and let them do the work. To get the most from the experience, have an idea about what outfits you'd like before you go. There's no obligation to buy and most services are free.

in which to build up confidence again and move out into the world wearing a genuine smile. And your self-image is the place to start.

The best thing about this idea is that I'm not going to suggest diets or exercise! Instead I think it's time to indulge in a bit of good old-fashioned retail therapy. During the divorce, fashion was probably the least of your worries. But now you're free to move on and create a new you, and fashion is an excellent tool to help.

Many people coming out of long marriages have slipped into some bad habits when it comes to their personal style. So some of us need a complete fashion shake-up and others just need to be encouraged to try something new.

Bringing up children and looking after a home, or taking part in the daily grind of office life, makes it easy to fall into a fashion rut. You have your work clothes and your leisure clothes. You've probably got your party clothes, too. But let's face it, everyone's seen that little black dress so many times now it could go to the party without you, and your best shirt's almost frayed it's seen so much wear! If this sounds like your wardrobe, then now's the time to have a bit of fashionable fun.

WHAT'S LURKING IN YOUR WARDROBE?

The first thing you need to do when revamping your wardrobe is to become brutal. You're probably a little tougher now than you were at the start of the divorce, so why not use it to your advantage? Start with a delve into your drawers. Then take everything out of the closets and lay it all on the bed. Anything you haven't worn in the past year goes straight in the charity bag. And you can't be sentimental. That old Laura Ashley dress you wore to your cousin's wedding really won't be worn again, and the skintight Levis you've had since the seventies are probably just obscene. So get rid of them!

Throw out any old and holey underwear, mismatched socks, and anything that's damaged. Color code the remaining clothes and divide them into categories—working, relaxing, going out, and day-to-day will get you started. This way you can see if a pattern emerges. Do you own more leggings than the cast of *Fame*? Have you got fourteen suits for work but only one pair of pants for parties? Maybe all your clothes are better suited to gardening than getting back into the dating game? By doing this you can see where you need to concentrate your efforts.

Let's face it, after a divorce it's unlikely that you're going to feel flush with cash. So, pick just one area of your wardrobe that needs augmenting or updating and that way you'll avoid wasting money on things you don't need. Your color coding will show that another black top is just going to overcrowd the family of eight you've already got.

Worried about the body that's underneath the clothes? Then have a look at IDEA 25, *Body beautiful*, and feel great about yourself.

Try another idea . . .

"I base my fashion taste on what doesn't itch!"
GILDA RADNER

Defining idea . . .

Use the color and theme codes to find out clues about what you need and where some potential changes could be made: if everything in your wardrobe is black, why not experiment with a bit of color? You don't have to go wild at first—try a tie or a scarf to give you confidence. If all your shoes are sensible and brown, why not buy something completely different? There's a huge array of sneaker-type leisure shoes available that are comfortable and practical, but eminently fashionable.

Take someone you trust with you when you go shopping, but why not take someone whose fashion sense you really admire rather than your mom?

Q **How can I start to wear skirts when my husband said I had fat legs?**

How did it go?

A *You are no longer with your husband and his views no longer matter. Ask friends you trust to come with you and try on some skirts. Gauge their reaction. Try ones that skim your figure rather than cling and wear them on the knee or just below for the most flattering effect. You'll look great!*

Q **Can men use a personal shopping service?**

A *Yes. It's an excellent way for men to update their look without getting fed up with the shopping process. You can go on your own and still get an expert opinion about what suits you.*

47

Sports car psychology

Do you feel life's passing you by? Fancy a Ferrari? Let's look at why you're itching to put your foot down and explore the need for midlife speed. It can seriously damage your marital health.

This time of life is a real danger zone for affairs as we attempt to rekindle the feelings of youth and excitement that seem lacking in our lives. Porsches, plastic surgery, and a penchant for speed can swiftly follow, but so can divorce.

LIFE IN THE SLOW LANE

The term "midlife crisis" seems a rather harsh way of describing people between the ages of forty and fifty who've ever had the desire to reevaluate their lives. However, it's often given as the reason why so many people in this age bracket divorce.

Here's an idea for you . . .

Have a look at these questions to see if you lust after life in the fast lane:

- **Do you suddenly feel discontent with your life and lifestyle?**
- **Are you bored with aspects of your life that used to be fulfilling?**
- **Are you feeling the need for adventure or a change of scenery?**
- **Are you questioning the path of your life and your life choices?**
- **Are you fearful of the future?**
- **Do you feel trapped?**

If you've answered yes to any of them, don't panic or rush out to the car showroom. Instead use the realization you could be having a midlife crisis to analyze your life. Highlight the areas you're unhappy with and work out how you can make them better. Could you change your job? Rejuvenate your marriage? Try an alternative lifestyle? Avoiding snap decisions but making informed lifestyle changes will ensure you'll make the transition into the next part of your life perfectly.

Images of balding men leaving their wives and buying Porsches, or middleaged women driving their boy-toys around in convertibles are popular with the media and are looked on with disdain. But why is it many of us reach our middle years and become desperate for something new and exciting?

The middle years of life can be the first time we come to terms with our mortality. Maybe a health scare or the death of a parent acts as the trigger and provokes a reassessment of everything in our lives. The most common feature to receive this scrutiny is our relationships. Marriages that have previously seemed fulfilling and even stimulating suddenly seem dull and lifeless, and we feel a primal urge to move on to pastures new.

SWITCH TO THE FAST LANE

Rather than see this process of life transition in the negative terms of a midlife crisis, I prefer to see it as "sports car psychology." Think about it: You've got a need for something new and exciting in your life, a desire to accelerate out of your boring routine and into the fast lane of fun—quite literally, you want to buy a sports car!

So, what can you do about it? Should you in fact do anything about it? Why not just put your foot down and roar into the future with style? Whatever you choose to do, you must remember that it is just that—a choice. To make the best choice for you, it's a good idea to have a look at exactly what underpins these feelings.

Maybe you don't want a sports car, but you would like to try something new and exciting? Have a look at IDEA 37, *And now, time for something completely different*, and put some fun into your future.

Try another idea . . .

Facing your own mortality can be a shock that gets you thinking. You've been in the same marriage or job for fifteen years or more, and nothing much is likely to change. Perhaps your children are grown and you feel that your role as a parent is redundant. Maybe your kids' lives seem exciting and filled with the opportunities you long for. Or maybe you even want to sleep with someone young and attractive to feel that way yourself. All these things suddenly seem urgent and must be done before it's too late.

If you have the money, it can actually be an exciting and positive choice to buy a sports car—it's probably safer than having an affair! And after years of trundling around in a family sedan full of dogs, kids, and groceries, climbing into a coupe can be an exhilarating way to blow the cobwebs from your life.

"There is more to life than increasing its speed."
GANDHI

Defining idea . . .

Understanding where the feelings of discontent and boredom that can typify sports car psychology come from is key to making the best decisions for the rest of your life. It's easy to feel that other people's lives are better than yours or that their marriages are more fulfilling, but it's equally as likely that this is just your view and not the real situation. Perhaps your marriage *is* stale; maybe it *is* time for a divorce. Perhaps even after you've bought the sports car you may still need to rev through the gears toward ultimate life satisfaction. But with a little awareness you may also be able to give your relationship a full service and save it from the scrap heap.

How did it go?

Q   Is a midlife crisis a real psychological condition?

A   *Many people feel it's a concept society has created. But the feelings associated with it are very real. Discontent and boredom with life can often lead to long-term marital problems, so it's important to treat your feelings with respect.*

Q   I'm fifty and just bought a sports car. Does that mean I'm having a midlife crisis?

A   *Not at all: it could just mean you like cars. If everything in your life and relationship is going well, then simply relax and enjoy it.*

48

Will you, or won't you?

Making a will is necessary for everyone and absolutely essential if you're divorced and you don't want your ex to get your every last penny. Follow this no-fuss guide to making yours—don't come back and haunt your partner!

Many people put off making a will because they don't want to think about death. They feel it's morbid and maybe even tempting fate. Of course this isn't the case, and making a will is as much a part of life as it is of death. Unlike a divorce, making a will can be a very quick and painless procedure, so don't put it off!

WHAT'S IN A WILL?

A will is a legal document that designates the transfer of your assets after your death. You must be over eighteen years old and of sound mental capacities to make

Here's an idea for you . . .

If you can't face the thought of yet another appointment with your attorney so soon after the divorce, make your will online. There are a number of services that offer legally binding ways to make your last will and testament and many of them do so in a user-friendly way. If you don't have access to the Internet at home, visit an Internet café and browse for the service that suits you. Avoid anything that seems confusing or very complicated, and don't part with any money until you're happy with the service they are providing. Also make sure you find a service that's legally binding in your country of domicile. Personal recommendations can help with this, as can a quick email or phone call to the service provider to check out any queries.

your will and it has to be signed by independent witnesses. Essentially, a will is your way of choosing who will benefit from your assets when you are no longer around to enjoy them. Why let the state take that benefit away from your loved ones and claim your estate simply because you were too scared to make a will?

It's a myth that you have to be rich to make a will. They have become simple and inexpensive to draw up over recent years, therefore making them accessible to everybody. Every will is different and personal but each one will include some or all of the following aspects:

- Your name and address
- A brief inventory of your assets
- The names of your spouse and children
- A list of your beneficiaries and what assets you wish them to receive
- Alternative named beneficiaries if their death precedes yours
- Details of specific gifts of smaller items
- The establishment of legal trusts
- Cancellation of any debts owed to you if you wish
- How you wish for any applicable taxes to be paid

- The name of the will's executor
- Names of guardians for your minor children
- Your signature
- Your witnesses' signatures

Is your will just another one of your financial worries? Maybe you're tempted to spend all you've got anyway? Have a look at IDEA 35, *Save it or spend it?*, for some sensible advice.

Try another idea . . .

An "executor" is simply the name given to the person or authority who will oversee the practicalities of turning your will into reality.

You can choose your executor, who will normally be a spouse, an adult child, a friend, relative, or in some cases a bank, attorney, or legal trust. In the case of the latter category a fee will usually be paid for this service out of the value of the estate.

WILLS AND DIVORCE

Throughout your life it may be necessary to update or change the contents of your will. Almost everyone who has gotten divorced will not want their ex-spouse to be the major beneficiary of their estate. It's therefore vital to change your will during or after your divorce proceedings. This is easily done as long as you follow some simple procedures. You must write your new will, sign it, and get it witnessed and notarized before it can be viewed as a legal document. And although the most recent will is usually taken to be the legally binding document, it makes things much simpler if any previous wills are destroyed.

It's also necessary to make a will if you have divorced your spouse and are now living with a new partner. Unlike if you were married, your new partner will not be legally entitled to

"Where there's a will, there's a way."
TRADITIONAL SAYING

Defining idea . . .

209

inherit anything from your estate unless you will it to them. This is the case even if you've been living together as man and wife for a number of years, and it's best to get your wishes down on paper to avoid any disputes in the future.

Disputes over wills can often occur in the case of divorce and remarriage, or cohabitation, when the new partner receives the bulk of the estate rather than it going to the children of the previous marriage. Make very sure you know who you want your beneficiaries to be and exactly what you wish them to receive after your death. Include their full names as well as their relationship to you. Keep your will in a safe place, but make sure your friends or family know where to find it.

How did it go?

Q **What details will I need to complete my will online?**

A *You'll need all the basics, like the names of beneficiaries and what you wish them to receive, plus an accurate inventory of your assets, which will include property, up-to-date details of your accounts, investments, and savings as well as any life insurance policies you might have. Also feel free to note down any small but sentimental items you wish to bequeath.*

Q **What does it mean if a will is in probate?**

A *Quite simply this means that a will is in a kind of legal clearing process. Probate determines whether a will is legally valid before it becomes finalized. The term comes from the Latin word meaning "to prove."*

49

Within reach

You're nearly there! It's simply a matter of time before your divorce is official, but does that mean you're still married?

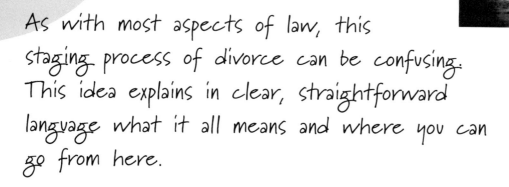

As with most aspects of law, this staging process of divorce can be confusing. This idea explains in clear, straightforward language what it all means and where you can go from here.

THE WAITING GAME

So much of divorce seems to involve waiting. You wait for appointments with attorneys, for petitions to go through, for judgments to be made, and for final decisions to be reached. Sometimes it seems the process will never end and you'll be stuck in the limbo land of divorce forever.

The most common reason that you'll need to wait a while for your divorce to be granted is finance. It doesn't take long to realize that most things to do with divorce revolve around financial matters, and this is no exception. In some cases the divorce may be granted before the full financial settlement is reached, but it's usual

Here's an idea for you . . .

Plan how to mark the occasion. If you're happy about getting divorced then celebrate with some friends. If you're unhappy about it, get some friends to commiserate with you. If you don't feel up to doing that, write an entry in your diary or take some time to grieve a little with some photographs. Allowing yourself to make this a notable event is a healthy and cathartic way to deal with the stress of your divorce.

for the final papers of the divorce to come hand in hand with the final agreement on money matters.

Unfortunately if you can't agree on a financial settlement with your spouse, you may need to attend a number of court hearings to resolve the matter. This can put the finalization of your divorce back a number of months. The other vital issue that needs to be agreed on before the divorce is granted is the provisions for your children. However, once the courts are assured that a fair financial agreement has been made and the best interests of the children have been reached, then your final papers will be on their way.

THE BEGINNING OF THE END

People going through a divorce experience a range of emotional reactions as the final decree gets closer. To some it's a cause for celebration, but to others it's a cause of great sadness. You're not alone in this reaction if you do feel sad. The end of a marriage is a difficult thing to accept. Your life has diverted from the path it was on, and it's normal to find that scary and upsetting. So, try to be kind to yourself, and don't feel you have to put on a brave face if you don't want to.

Even if you do feel depressed about the situation, there are ways to work through it positively. So, how can you prepare yourself for the beginning of the end of your marriage? Well, you start by taking things step by step. You know that the final papers are on the way, so plan for it. Let your friends or family know it will be a difficult day for you, and tell them what you need in terms of support. It's much easier for people to support you if you tell them how they can do so.

Tell them if you need some space to come to terms with this by yourself. Or, if you need company, have them primed to come around with drinks and sympathy. If you can't face work, then take the day off and concentrate on making yourself feel

Want to prepare for the next stage? Then take a look at IDEA 51, *Absolute freedom*, and start ticking off the days.

Try another idea . . .

"My D-I-V-O-R-C-E becomes final today!"
TAMMY WYNETTE

Defining idea . . .

better. But don't face the day entirely on your own if you can help it. Of course, you must have some private time, but also try to see a friend or talk to someone on the phone. That way you won't feel so alone.

Your divorce is becoming a reality, and realities are always much easier to deal with than "what-ifs?" Stay strong and see the this process as the first step toward your new life.

How did it go?

Q **Can I stop my divorce after the petition has been accepted?**

A *Yes. Until the final decree is pronounced, the divorce proceedings can be stopped. Contact your attorney for further advice.*

50

The divorce hall of fame

Divorce can happen to anyone, from the boy and girl next door to a prince and princess. Let's take a look at some of the divorces that rocked the world. Why did these marriages fail, and can we learn any lessons from their mistakes?

It seems news of a celebrity divorce hits the papers every day. So, why is it that people in the public eye seem more prone to divorce than the rest of us? Are they just seeking attention, or does a media marriage suffer more pressures than a regular one?

A ROYAL DECREE

When divorce was granted on August 28, 1996, the process that broke the fairy-tale marriage between the Prince and Princess of Wales was completed. Charles had cheated with Camilla Parker Bowles, his long-term lover, and Diana had cheated with James Hewitt, her knight in shining armor.

Here's an idea for you . . .

Take a look at the famous divorces that interest you and isolate why you think the relationships failed. Look at the issues of fame, beauty, family, adultery, money, alcohol, and drugs and see what impact they had. Then apply the lessons you've learned to your own relationship. Is it under pressure in any way? Can you see a key in the relationships of the famous that could unlock the solution to your own marital problems? For example, Tom Cruise and Nicole Kidman's relationship may have crumbled because they both had international careers. An investment banker friend of mine and his lawyer wife had exactly the same problem, but it was only when they saw their relationship problems mirrored by a famous couple that they were able to identify the problem clearly.

The media spotlight blazed on the pair as they discussed their indiscretions and marriage breakup on national TV. Diana, comfortable in the media glare, gave her heart-wrenching "Queen of Hearts" speech and Charles, less comfortable, looked grave and disappointed during his Dimbleby interview.

But who really was at fault? Diana talked openly about her problems with Charles and her feelings of isolation inside the most famous family in the world. She discussed her bulimia, her thwarted love for Charles and, most shockingly, his affair with Camilla and hers with Hewitt. Her marriage, she said, had been doomed from the start. There were, after all, three of them in it. But she certainly added to the numbers when she took her own lover. Was her adultery negated by his?

What can we learn from this? If we marry each other for love, then we have a fighting chance of staying the course. As a child I remember nineteen-year-old Diana, coy and dressed in royal blue, proclaiming her love for Charles.

My parents, however, remember Charles, older and far more experienced, blustering at the question "Are you in love?" His answer, "Whatever that means!" has since been analyzed more than the atom.

Have a look at IDEA 1, *Once upon a time . . .*, to find out why fairy-tale marriages can often end in the nightmare of divorce.

Try another idea . . .

So, maybe Charles wasn't the fairy-tale prince that Diana or the public expected. But then he was under enormous pressure to marry a suitable girl and produce suitable heirs. And Camilla, though he loved her, was not suitable. Diana was. With the media pressure, the family pressure, and even the public pressure on the couple, was there really any chance of their union lasting? Maybe not, but we can learn from their mistakes.

THE CASE OF THE "MUCH MARRIEDS"

The royal divorce is not the only marriage to begin and end in the spotlight and suffer because of it. Hollywood and movie marriages are notorious for their short-lived status. Zsa Zsa Gabor has quipped endlessly about her nine marriages, Mickey Rooney lost his innocent appeal with eight, Lana Turner married seven times, and many of today's stars lose much of their glow in the divorce courts. Jennifer Lopez is quickly becoming a modern "much-married," filing for divorce from her second husband after only ten months. Although glamorous, sad, and disappointing in many ways, these celebrities have always believed enough in love to try again.

"How many husbands have I had? You mean apart from my own?"
ZSA ZSA GABOR

Defining idea . . .

217

So, why is celebrity divorce so common? Well, the pressures of a private life in public are huge. Pressure causes cracks, and the same is true of a normal relationship. The more pressure you put it under, the more scrutiny it has to face from outside forces, friends, and relatives, the more cracks appear.

The pressures faced by celebrity marriages can tell us much about our own relationships. Diana found living without the support of a family almost too much to bear. The royals were cold and critical and her own parents were divorced and far away. When a relationship starts to crumble, sometimes a strong family unit can hold it together. In the princess's case this was an empty hope.

Adultery is a key reason for celebrity divorce and simply mirrors the temptations of the rest of us. Fidelity is key to trust and without trust a relationship fails. Celebrities living in the world of the "beautiful people" are probably more tempted than most, but resisting the urge to stick your hand in a sweet pot of honey will also stop you from getting stung by wasps. And divorce certainly has a nasty sting!

Q How can famous divorces help me? They're not under the kind of financial pressure I am!

How did it go?

A *Financial pressure is often a key issue in many celebrity breakups. Famous men have gone bankrupt and their wives have left them. Famous women have earned more than their husbands and the men look elsewhere. Money really does make the world of relationships turn, so have a look again and see what lessons you can find.*

Q How can I feel less threatened by the beautiful women my husband works with?

A *Celebrities face this all the time. Everyone is gorgeous and everyone is a temptation. Remember that your husband has chosen to marry you, not one of his attractive colleagues. Gain confidence from that and don't allow your insecurities to dominate the relationship. Talk to him of your fears, but also accept his love.*

51

Absolute freedom

Your final decree has come through and that means you're fully divorced. But is it time for congratulations or commiserations? If absolute freedom doesn't float your boat, here's how to move on.

Many people have mixed reactions on receiving their final decree. Even those who have been longing for it to land in the mailbox can feel sad and empty when it finally does.

COPING WITH COMPLETION

Some of us have been drained emotionally and financially by the process and the final decree can simply be a reminder of how much the divorce has cost. So, how can we move forward into the freedom and excitement of our future if all we're feeling is drained, hurt, and rejected?

Use one or more of the six suggestions below to celebrate your freedom and take a step toward doing something new with your freedom:

- **Take a trip somewhere you've always wanted to go**
- **Visit and spend time with your family and accept their support**
- **Indulge in something frivolous just because you can**
- **Redecorate your house in the way you want**
- **Sign up for classes in something that interests you**
- **See a nutritionist or alternative therapist and kick start your new healthy lifestyle**

I won't pretend it's easy, but the fact remains that you have survived so far and you can survive the next stage, too. You've gone through the financial and emotional turmoil of your divorce and come out in one piece at the other end. That in itself means you have all the ingredients to make a happy and exciting future.

Think about it: You're resilient, you're strong, you've gained a depth of life experience you never had before, and you've realized that you won't die from a broken heart. In fact you now know that a broken heart is like any other broken part of the body—given time and care, it mends.

Even if you're happy to be divorced and are excited about the prospect of a free and single future, it can be confusing if you feel empty and alone when the final decree comes through. It's important to realize that this is a normal reaction. This signifies the end of one stage of your life. And all endings can be a little sad, so allow yourself time to process the information. One phase of your life may have ended, but a new one has begun.

TIE UP THE LOOSE ENDS

If you are feeling empty or at a loss as to what to do next, it may come as a pleasant surprise to know that there are a few loose ends of your marriage to tie up even after the divorce is final. If you can't wait to get out and party, then this may seem a bit of a chore.

First of all, it's important to read and file away all the papers relevant to your divorce. It's especially important to keep your final decree safe, as you'll need this should you ever wish to remarry, or if you need to prove you're divorced (for example, if you're female and you want to apply for a passport in your maiden name).

Although the decree will mention that your ex-spouse does not have the same claim to your property and assets after your death as they did when you were married, it's important to revise your will. This may not seem like a pleasant thing to do, but it is necessary if you wish the contents of your will to change in any way after the divorce.

There are lots of fussy and rather irritating things to sort out, but once they are done you may feel a sense of closure that was absent simply with the arrival of the legal certificate.

Need a bit of extra help moving on? Look at IDEA 52, *Happily ever after*, and make your future a happy one.

Try another idea . . .

"Freedom is what you do with what's been done to you."
JEAN PAUL SARTRE

Defining idea . . .

So, close all your joint bank accounts and transfer the money in them as agreed in your financial settlement. Remember to cancel your joint credit cards and joint gym and club memberships. If the marital home has been awarded to one spouse, take the other's name off the mortgage agreement or the property deeds. Set up your own bank accounts and arrange to see an independent financial advisor if you need to.

Use this opportunity to tie up your emotional loose ends as well. First of all, accept that the relationship is finally over. The receipt of the final certificate can be a good way to come to terms with this. Allow yourself time to grieve if necessary or mark the occasion with a celebration. Dismiss thoughts of revenge or punishment for your partner, as this will only keep you in the past. Instead, use this moment to reevaluate your priorities and put yourself and your children above any guilt, grief, or hurt you feel over a dead relationship.

Your divorce papers are your passport to freedom and a new life. Sit down and decide where you want to go, and make sure that wherever you travel your new destination is somewhere you really want to be.

Q   Can I appeal against the final financial settlement?

A   Usually, it is just that—final. But in some cases there is an appeal system. You may be able to challenge maintenance or child support payments if the circumstances of you or your ex have changed. For example, if one of you has remarried or you've lost your job. Take legal advice to be certain.

Q   Can I continue to use my married name now that my divorce is final?

A   Yes you can. If you do wish to change it back to your maiden name, you will need a copy of your final decree and your birth certificate. This is also relevant for passports, driving licences, and bank accounts.

How did it go?

52

Happily ever after

Welcome to the rest of your life! The nightmare is now over and it's time to wake up to your future. From this point onward, you should focus on the new you and where you want to go so you can write your own happy ending.

Maybe your married life hasn't worked out quite the way you thought it would when you said "I do." But at least you've successfully negotiated the minefield of saying "I don't." And although you can't change the past, you can choose your future.

GENERATION EX

Every generation is defined in some way. The women of the nineteen-twenties were known as the flappers, the children that filled the maternity wards of the postwar years are known as the baby boomers, and the go-getters of the eighties as yuppies.

Here's an idea for you . . .

Try writing about your experiences. Surviving divorce is something to be applauded. Doing so and emerging with a greater understanding of yourself and those around you is even better. You know you'll use this experience to positively shape your future, so put it down on paper. Or you could try a web log–known as a blog–to chart your experiences online. Not only will it help you remember what you've learned, it will also be a cathartic way to move on, and it could even help others. Check out www.blogger.com for advice to get you started.

So, what will we modern divorce survivors be known as? Some have described the generation spanning the nineties and beyond as Generation X. Generation Ex would be a more accurate description. With over one in two marriages dissolving in tears in the US and similar or worse statistics worldwide, there are few members of this generation who haven't come into contact with divorce.

However, with the increase in divorces, society has become more tolerant of those who have been through it. Divorcees are no longer stigmatized and reviled. In fact, many regard those who have been through a separation and divorce as being wiser and more experienced because of it.

Although divorce can be a harsh and heartbreaking process, it shouldn't be seen as the end of anything else but a marriage. Just because your marriage has ended it doesn't mean your quest for a happy ending has to as well. But it is now up to you to write it. You've survived your divorce and you're standing on the brink of your future. Maybe you need just a little push to jump right in.

FUTURE FOCUS

You will have used up a great deal of mental and physical energy in the course of your divorce. Now that it's over, you've got the chance to recharge your batteries and direct your energy toward the positive experiences that will make up your future.

I believe that everyone can achieve the happiness he or she wishes for, even after divorce. Divorce does not kill our capacity for love. It may make us more wary of how we bestow it and more cautious of committing ourselves. A little caution, though, will save us from rebound affairs and further heartbreak.

We can choose our happy ending and work toward it. One of the tricks for doing this is not to live in the past. You're single now, so think single. That's not a negative thing. It means you can make your own plans, make your own choices, and live your own life. And if or when you choose to share your life with someone again you'll be far more aware of who you are and what you need. These are key elements in making new relationships work and have come directly from what you've learned during your divorce.

Your marriage breakup has taught you that life is a challenge and you don't always get what you expect. But it has also shown you have the strength of character to deal with whatever life throws at you. See this as liberating and exhilarating self-knowledge that will ensure you will make positive choices and changes in the future.

Still not quite ready for "happily ever after"? Have a look at IDEA 51, *Absolute freedom*, and you soon will be.

Try another idea . . .

"Happiness is a choice that requires effort at times."
ANONYMOUS

Defining idea . . .

229

You know now that life isn't a fairy tale, so you won't expect a Prince Charming or an innocent princess in the future. And you also know that even nightmares end, so you won't expect your bad times to go on forever. This will give you the ability to enter a new relationship with greater insight than you had when you first got married, and therefore a greater chance of a successful relationship.

Divorce is really a process of transition from being married back to being single. Transition brings change and it's important to accept and learn from that change rather than being scared of it. Get rid of any lingering negative emotions that might get in the way of your happy ending.

How did it go?

Q How can I set up a blog?

A *You'll need to have Internet access and some web space. Your Internet service provider can provide you with the space that will enable you to get started. You'll need an Internet address for your site so people can access it and then you can get writing. Or, you can use one of the many free blog host sites. Post a regular account of your experiences online and, if you want, allow people to email their responses to the site.*

Q How can I get my happy ending when divorcees are more likely to divorce again if they remarry?

A *Some statistics do suggest this to be true, but why view yourself as just another number? You can choose your future. Use everything you have learned in your divorce to create your happy ending and to make sure you don't make the same mistakes again.*

Where it's at...

52 Brilliant Ideas

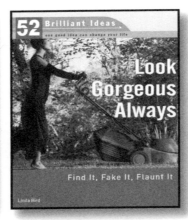

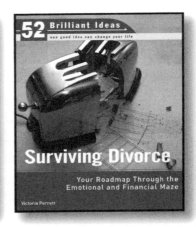

LIVE LONGER
978-0-399-53302-0 • 0-399-53302-8

LOOK GORGEOUS ALWAYS
978-0-399-53304-4 • 0-399-53304-4

SURVIVING DIVORCE
978-0-399-53305-1 • 0-399-53305-2

INCREDIBLE ORGASMS
978-0-399-53303-7 • 0-399-53303-6

DETOX YOUR FINANCES
978-0-399-53301-3 • 0-399-53301-X

**GET MARRIED
WITHOUT A HITCH**
978-0-399-53306-8 • 0-399-53306-0

PERIGEE An imprint of Penguin Group (USA)